Outlines of a
Philosophy of Art

By

R. G. Collingwood

LONDON
Oxford University Press
Humphrey Milford
1925

Republished 1976
Scholarly Press, Inc., 22929 Industrial Drive East
St. Clair Shores, Michigan 48080

Oxford University Press
London   Edinburgh   Glasgow   Copenhagen
New York   Toronto   Melbourne   Cape Town
Bombay   Calcutta   Madras   Shanghai
Humphrey Milford Publisher to the UNIVERSITY

Printed in England

PREFACE

THIS book aims at doing two things : stating a general conception of art, and developing its consequences. The general conception here maintained is not new ; it is one already familiar from the works of Coleridge, Croce, and many others ; it is the view that art is at bottom neither more nor less than imagination. But when one has arrived at such a conception, the question is what to do next. One may advertise its merits by applying it to numerous examples and showing how neatly it fits them ; but this soon degenerates into a conjuring trick which the audience has seen through. Or one may criticize other people's views ; but this is apt to be a mere washing of dirty linen in public. Or one may frankly begin talking about something else, and fill up the book with observations on art and artists. There remains a more difficult course : to develop the conception itself in such a way as to lay bare the implications contained in it. This is perhaps the only course that deserves the name of philosophy. For philosophy lives in its own details ; and it ought to treat each detail as a fresh problem, with a place of its own in the general body of philosophical thought, and not as another lock to be opened with the same skeleton key, or as one which for that very reason is not worth opening.

There are certain subordinate conceptions contained within the general conception of art : the sublime, the comic, and the forms of beauty in general ; the antitheses of nature and art, formal art and naturalistic art, classical and romantic art, genius and taste, matter and form ; notions like that of technique ; distinctions between the various so-called arts ; and the like. To reduce these to so many cases of art, and to leave it at that, is to fall a victim to the skeleton-key habit, to convert the philosophy of art into a night in which all cows are black. These conceptions have their own value in their own place, and it ought to be possible not only to admit this fact in the abstract but to demonstrate it by showing what their place is : which means showing them to be involved in the conception of art as such, to be distinctions into which that conception articulates itself.

The greater part of the following essay is an attempt to carry out this programme. The general conception of art and of its place in life, here stated in the first and last chapters, has been formulated in the writer's book called *Speculum Mentis* ; but the other chapters are concerned with these detailed articulations, which the plan of the earlier work perforce excluded.

The result is no more than an outline. Comparatively few of the possible topics have been discussed, and those as briefly as possible, with little in the way of illustration or explanation ; while criticism and reference to the history of the subject have been altogether excluded. But the attempt to cover much ground in few words is an attempt always worth making ; and if the result is found worth reading, the reader as well as the writer must thank the Delegates of the Clarendon Press, without whose invitation the book would not have been written.

R. G. C.

Skipness,
August, 1924.

CONTENTS

The General Nature of Art

§ 1. *The Problem.*—The word art has in ordinary usage three senses. First, it means the creation of objects or the pursuit of activities called works of art, by people called artists ; these works being distinguished from other objects and acts not merely as human products, but as products intended to be beautiful. Secondly, it means the creation of objects or the pursuit of activities called artificial as opposed to natural ; that is to say objects created or activities pursued by human beings consciously free to control their natural impulses and to organize their life on a plan. Thirdly, it means that frame of mind which we call artistic, the frame of mind in which we are aware of beauty.

This is not a mere linguistic accident or an ambiguity in the word art. There is a real relation between the three things enumerated above, which is revealed by the fact that the first is the sum of the second and third. Art, in the sense in which we call sculpture or music an art, differs from art in the sense in which agriculture or navigation is an art in one point only : namely in being controlled or dominated by art in the sense of the awareness of beauty.

Since the controlling element in the so-called ' arts ' of sculpture, music and the rest is the awareness of beauty, the central notion in the philosophy of art is the notion of a specific activity by which we apprehend objects as beautiful. Fundamentally, fine art is this apprehension of beauty. Where this is present, it will find out a way to create objects which shall express itself ; where it is absent, no degree of technical skill in the creation of objects will take its place or conjure it into existence. The awareness of beauty is at once the starting-point and the culmination, the presupposition and the end, of all art. His awareness of beauty is the initial impulse in obedience to which a painter begins to paint a picture; it is by this same awareness that he decides, at every moment of the process, what to do to his picture next; and it is simply an enlargement and a sharpening of the same awareness that constitute, either for him or for anyone else, the value of the picture when it is done.

The philosophy of art is the attempt to discover what art is; and this involves not an examination of the world around us in order to discover and analyse instances of it, as if it were a chemical substance, but a reflection upon our own activities, among which art has its place. But if there are three different activities that go by the name of art, which of these do we propose to investigate? The answer is, that if the three senses of the word art are connected by a real and necessary bond, the philosophy of art cannot confine itself to any one of them, to the exclusion of the others. It must begin by studying that which is most fundamental, the awareness of beauty; it must go on to study the distinction between the natural and the artificial, and to show how this distinction arises; and it must end by studying that special form of production in which the artificial object is a work of art. And it must justify this programme by showing that its three parts are connected in such a way that they cannot be understood separately.

But art is only one of a number of activities; and to answer the question what art is can only mean placing it in its relation to our other activities. Hence the only possible philosophy of art is a general philosophy of man and his world with special reference to man's function as an artist and his world's aspect of beauty.

In this case, as in all other cases, the form and order of the exposition must in a sense invert the form and order of inquiry. In trying to arrive at an understanding of any activity, one must begin with a mass of experience relative to that activity; and this experience cannot be acquired by philosophical thinking, or by scientific experiments, or by observation of the activity in other people, but only by a long and specialized pursuit of the activity itself. Only after this experience has been acquired is it possible to reflect upon it and bring to light the principles underlying it. To expound the philosophy of an activity is to expound these principles in their general character and their implications ; and such an exposition may deceive unwary readers into thinking that the writer is trying to deduce the features of a certain field of activity altogether *a priori* and in abstraction from actual experience, when he is really trying to communicate his reflections upon his own experience to readers who have been through the same experience themselves.

§ 2. *Art in its Generic Nature.*—For the present, then, art is to mean the special activity by which we apprehend beauty. This implies that there are various activities of which we have experience, and that art has certain features in common with them all and others peculiar to itself; to determine its general nature therefore involves distinguishing its generic nature on the one hand and its specific nature on the other. Definition, according to the principles of formal logic, must proceed by genus and differentia.

It is important to make this distinction at the outset, because reflection upon activities like art or religion very often frustrates itself by confusing a generic with a specific feature. Every activity is in certain ways very much like any other ; and people who are trying to describe their own experience of art, religion, science and so forth constantly select for emphasis features due not to the special character of the activity but to the fact that they have had special experience of it. For instance, religion is described as giving knowledge of ultimate reality, which is precisely what artists claim for art, scientists for science, and philosophers for philosophy ; or as giving a sense of victory over one's lower nature, of peace, of security, which are feelings involved in any activity whatever, provided it is pursued earnestly and successfully ; and so forth. The same error, upon a larger scale, appears in the attempt to equate various activities with the three aspects of the mental life which are distinguished by analytic psychology : cognition, conation and emotion. This threefold distinction has a very real value, but it becomes a fantastic mythology if it is mistaken for a distinction between three activities which can exist separately, or of which one can predominate over the other, or of which one can undergo a modification without producing corresponding modifications in the other.

In every field of activity there is a theoretical element, in virtue of which the mind is aware of something ; there is a practical element in virtue of which the mind is bringing about a change in itself and in its world ; and there is an element of feeling, in virtue of which the mind's cognitions and actions are coloured with desire and aversion, pleasure and pain. In no case is any one of these elements active without the others ; they are correlative elements in every act and every experience, and make up a single indivisible whole. But the theoretical element is not always knowledge in the strict sense of the word ; knowledge is the highest form of theoretical activity, not equivalent to that activity in general : and in the same way moral action, though the highest form of practical activity, is not found wherever practical activity is found. And each specific form of theory, practice or feeling involves corresponding forms of the other two elements, and cannot exist in the absence of these.

Merely in virtue of its generic character as an activity, therefore, art is at once theoretical, practical and emotional. It is theoretical : that is, in art the mind has an object which it contemplates. But this object is an object of a specific kind, peculiar to itself ; it is not God, or natural law, or historical fact, or philosophical truth ; and because it is specifically different from the object of religion or science or history or philosophy, the act of contemplating it must also be a specifically peculiar kind of act. Art is practical: that is, in art the mind is trying to realize an ideal, to bring itself into a certain state and at the same time to bring its world into a certain state. But this ideal is not expediency or duty, and the mind's activity in art is therefore not a utilitarian or a moral activity. And again, art is emotional: that is, it is a life of pleasure and pain, desire and aversion, intertwined, as these opposite feelings always are, in such a way that each is conditioned by the felt or implied presence of the other. But these feelings are in the case of art tinged with a colour of their own ; the artist's pleasure is not the pleasure of the voluptuary or the scientist or the man of action, but a specifically aesthetic pleasure.

Art, religion, science, and so forth, which are here treated as species of a genus called activity, are in reality related to one another in a way which is not exactly that of co-ordinate species. This point will be taken up again and dealt with more fully in the last chapter. For the present it is sufficient to point out that the logic of genus and species is at this stage of the inquiry used as the first approximation to a truth which it does not exhaust.

§ 3. *Art in its Specific Nature : Theoretically, as Imagination.*— In art there are always a subject and an object, a contemplator and something contemplated. But the subject's activity, the object's nature, and the character of the relation between them have certain peculiarities which distinguish the case of art from other cases. What the subject does is to imagine : the object is an imaginary object, and the relation between them is that the individual or empirical act of imagining creates the object. In knowledge, on the other hand, the object is real ; and the relation between them is that the empirical act of knowing presupposes the object and does not create it. This may be said without prejudice to the idealistic view that there is an absolute or transcendental sense in which knowing creates its object ; for no idealist is so innocent as to confuse knowledge with imagination and to suppose that what we generally call knowing is simply imagining.

The object, in the case of art, is an imaginary object, not a real object. Shakespeare's printed text is a real object, and really lies before me; but to contemplate the tragedy of *Hamlet* is not to perceive this printed book but to ' see ' Hamlet himself as Shakespeare ' saw ' him. This ' seeing ' is the contemplation of a human character, human words, human actions; but the character, words, and actions of an imaginary human being. No doubt the story of Hamlet is derived from that of Olaf Cuaran; but Hamlet himself is not Olaf Cuaran but an imaginary person ultimately suggested by Olaf Cuaran. Consequently our own attitude towards Hamlet is that we do not know him, we imagine him. If we say that we know Hamlet to have killed his uncle, what we mean is either that we imagine him doing so, which is true, or that we know that Shakespeare imagined him doing so, which is also true, or that Hamlet was a real person who really did kill his uncle, which is untrue. Further, the Hamlet that we imagine is created by our act of imagining him; the Hamlet that Shakespeare imagined, by Shakespeare's act of imagining him; and these two Hamlets, though they may resemble each other, are not identical. Whereas the London that I know and the London that you know are the same London, and this London does not depend for its existence on your personal acquaintance with it, nor yet on mine.

But *Hamlet* would be neither more nor less of a great tragedy if, as might conceivably have happened, Olaf Cuaran had been just the kind of man, and had said and done just the things, that Shakespeare imagined Hamlet being and saying and doing. In that case the object would be real, and our imagining would apparently give place to knowing. But if art is imagining, does it not follow that the result would not be art?

It would follow, if the imaginary and the real excluded one another; and we certainly do use the word imaginary with a definite implication of unreality. But if I imagine Kubla Khan's palace in ' Xanadu ', this act is none the less an act of imagination because Shantu is a real town in China ; nor would it be any the less an act of imagination if it happened that the real Kubla Khan had really built such a palace there. To imagine an object is not to commit oneself in thought to its unreality ; it is to be wholly indifferent to its reality. An imaginary object, therefore, is not an unreal object but an object about which we do not trouble to ask whether it is real or unreal. The imaginary is not the opposite of the real, but the indifferent identity of the real and its opposite. Thus Shakespeare embodies history and fiction side by side in certain of his plays, but the plays are not mixtures of history and art, truth and beauty : they are art through and through, because the history and the fiction meet on equal terms ; for the purposes of the play the distinction between them is non-existent.

And yet we are quite right to oppose the imaginary to the real. For the real is only real as it stands in the real world ; and a fragment of history embedded in a work of fiction, by losing its real context and acquiring a fictitious context, becomes itself tainted with fiction. A lie that is half a truth becomes a lie throughout, because the false half infects the true half and twists it into a misrepresentation of the facts. Hence a work of art which indifferently includes fact and fiction becomes, by that mere indifference, pure fiction, though no doubt a fiction founded on fact.

To imagine is to refrain from making a distinction which we make whenever we think : the distinction between reality and unreality, truth and falsehood. Therefore imagining is not a kind of thinking, nor is thinking a kind of imagining, for each negates the specific nature of the other. Yet these two different activities are not wholly unrelated. Thinking is making a distinction between truth and falsehood; but this presupposes a phase of consciousness in which this distinction is not made. That which we deny or think false must be first imagined, or there is nothing to deny : that which we assert or think true must first be imagined, or else we could not ask whether it was true without assuming that it was true. Hence the relation between imagination and thought is that thought presupposes imagination, but imagination does not presuppose thought.

§ 4. *The Primitiveness of Art.*—This fact is of crucial importance for the attempt to determine the place of art in life as a whole. As thinking presupposes imagining, all those activities whose theoretical aspect takes the form of thought presuppose art ; and art is the basis of science, history, ' common sense ', and so forth. Art is the primary and fundamental activity of the mind, the original soil out of which all other activities grow. It is not a primitive form of religion or science or philosophy, it is something more primitive than these, something that underlies them and makes them possible.

This doctrine of the primitiveness of art runs counter to a certain view which was very widespread in the nineteenth century and still affects a great deal of our ordinary thinking : the view of art as an aristocratic activity, a higher and more specialized type of consciousness than perception of the ' commonsense ' world or religious or scientific thought. This notion encouraged a certain habit of self-adulation among artists, which went to great lengths in the aestheticism of the later nineteenth century ; and it would be difficult to quarrel with such an attitude if the philosophy on which it was founded were true, and if art really were a more highly-developed and logically advanced activity than others ; for in that case the artist would certainly be a spiritual aristocrat, related to other people as a mature man to children.

On the other hand, the doctrine of the primitiveness of art is slowly forcing itself upon us as we come to know more of the mental life of children and savages. We find that children who are quite incapable of advanced scientific and philosophical thinking constantly show a high degree of artistic power. Most children can extemporise verses and songs better than their elders; many of them invent excellent stories and draw in a peculiarly forcible and expressive way; and all without exception are at home in a region of imaginative make-believe from which the adult mind feels itself in some degree exiled. The same thing is true of savage and primitive races. The songs and stories, the drawings and carvings and dances of savage peoples are of an excellence quite disproportionate to the same peoples' knowledge and mastery of the world round them. These are familiar facts; but the philosophy which regards art as a highly-specialized activity is in plain conflict with them, and they are only intelligible on the view that art is a relatively primitive function of the mind.

A similar change of view has already taken place with regard to religion. Not many generations ago it was common to consider religion as an 'imposture', the fruit of a deliberate policy on the part of rulers, who constituted themselves priests in order to secure their hold over their subjects. That view fell before the recognition, which forced itself on people's minds as they came to know more about uncivilized man, that religion is a more primitive thing than policy, a thing that grows up of itself in the human mind long before that mind reaches the level of deliberate political thought. But we are still so far dominated by the corresponding error about art that we feel surprise at the artistic achievements of children and savages; and modern anthropology seeks for a religious motive in the art of palaeolithic man precisely as eighteenth-century philosophers sought for a political motive in the religious organization of primitive peoples.

To say that art is the primary activity of the mind implies that
art arises of itself and does not depend on the previous development of any other activity. It is not a kind of modified perception;
nor is it a kind of modified religion. It is on the contrary that of
which both perception and religion are modifications. When
a child playing on the shore says ' the water likes it when I dig
a river for it to run in ', he is not presupposing or assuming any
belief in a water-sprite ; he is performing an act of imagination
which is the basis upon which all beliefs of this kind are erected.
The fantasies of the poetic imagination are the material out of
which religion constructs its mythology, not vice versa. Most
current speculation about the origin of religion fails through not
recognizing that it presupposes poetic imagery ; and hence its
description of the mental processes involved in animism, magic,
and so forth, grotesquely distorts these things into some kind of
scientific theory, some analogical or inductive argument, whereas
they are at bottom simply imagination. Again, art is not based
upon a previous perception of real objects. We do not first
ascertain what the object really is and then modify it by allowing
our imagination to play upon it. We first imagine ; the attempt
to ascertain what the object really is involves the attempt to
criticize our own imaginations, and hence assumes that we have
already imagined.

The aestheticism which regards art as a higher activity than
perception or thought seems to be based on two motives. First,
it is due to the fact that to an adult and civilized man art is
difficult ; it costs him a struggle to put himself at the aesthetic
or imaginative point of view, and this struggle is taken for a struggle
towards a more highly-developed activity, whereas it is in fact
a struggle to recapture a more unsophisticated frame of mind.
The whole of our education is an education in facing facts ; it is
designed to lead us away from the world of imagination in which
the child lives, and to make us sober and habitual residents in the

world of perceptual objects. The child does not struggle to reach the imaginative point of view; he lives habitually in it; but the educated man cannot achieve it except by a struggle, because he must rid himself of the habits imposed upon him by his education, and think himself back into childhood. Secondly, aestheticism confuses the distinction between one kind of art and another with the distinction between art and something else. A view of art which is based exclusively on studying great works of art concludes naturally enough that art is a high and difficult thing, an aristocratic activity, to be approached only by people built on the scale of Dante and Michelangelo; and obviously it takes a greater man to write the *Paradiso* than to see that this is a pen and that twice two is four. But to compare trivial examples of thought—and what we call common sense is only thought at a comparatively trivial level—with great examples of art is not the way to a just comparison. Art includes both the *Paradiso* and a child's scribble or a guttersnipe's discordant whistle; thought includes both the multiplication table and the *Principia*, the perception of a pen and the *Decline and Fall*. If art, in its whole range from highest to lowest, is compared with the whole range of knowledge, the illusion disappears; it becomes clear enough that the artist as such is always a more unsophisticated and primitive spirit than the scientist as such; more of a child in his unstable emotional life, his inability to face facts and to organize his conduct rationally, his comparative crudity of outlook and comparative egotism of temper. Great artists overcome or compensate for these faults in so far as they are great, but continue to show them in so far as they are artists; the weaknesses of the artistic temperament are still visible in a Beethoven or a Dante, however they may be modified and transfigured by his greatness of soul.

Because art is a primitive thing, it does not follow that no one except the child and the savage can be an artist. The grown man

remains a child; and the civilized man remains a savage, so far as
he preserves any of that fresh and adventurous outlook on life
which maturity and civilization may seem to kill; and if, on
becoming grown up and civilized, a man really does lose this
freshness of heart, and allows himself to be overwhelmed by the
shades of the prison-house, then certainly the life of art is for him
at an end. But even this is only a temporary eclipse; maturity
and civilization have their own art, just because the spiritual life
is built on a basis of imagination and can never detach itself from
that basis.

On the other hand, the peculiar quality which belongs to the
child's art and the savage's art is an imaginative expression of
their own childish and savage life, and cannot exist away from
that life. To argue from the beauty of Greek vase-painting or
medieval sculpture to the conclusion that Greek or medieval life
as a whole was beautiful, harmonious, and enlightened, would be
as foolish as to suppose that a choir-boy with a beautiful voice
must be a model of the virtues, or the author of a Border ballad
a respectable citizen. The choir-boy is probably a young rascal,
and the author of the Border ballad was probably a brutal and
treacherous Border thief; and it is just because of that simplicity
and childishness which separates them from the morality of adult
civilized men that their art has so tender and innocent a beauty.
Educate them, civilize them, and their gift of song will mysteri-
ously vanish. If the Greeks had not been cruel, if the Middle
Ages had not been superstitious, the qualities which we find so
enchanting would not have been visible in their art. And this is
why we cannot emulate Greek vase-paintings and medieval
cathedrals, or revive our own folk-songs and country dances.
These things were once an integral part of a life which is not only
dead but which we would not revive if we could; as no one who
remembers his childhood would be a child again for the sake
of recapturing the childish keenness of imagination. If we want

to paint and build, sing and dance, we must find out how to do it for ourselves.

§ 5. *Art in its Specific Nature : Practically, as the Pursuit of Beauty.*—Art is imagination ; but imagination is an activity. To imagine is not simply to allow a train of images to drift idly across the mind, it is to make an effort to imagine, to work at imagination. One can imagine, as one can do anything else, well or ill ; and though one may do it well without taking trouble, one does it on the whole and in the long run better for trying to do it better.

To distinguish an activity as worse or better does not imply referring it to some standard other than itself. If we suspect ourselves of having thought wrongly, there is nothing to do but to think again ; thought cannot be checked except by further thought. Similarly, action can only be judged by reference to action. In no case can there be any criterion outside the activity itself, because, if there were, it would be only by this same activity that the criterion was recognized and applied. To imagine well means, therefore, to imagine imaginatively : to live up to a criterion contained in the activity itself. The ideal at which the act of imagining aims is simply the ideal of imagining. But that which art is the attempt to achieve is beauty ; and therefore the beautiful is neither more nor less than the imagined.

This implies that it is impossible to imagine anything that is not beautiful ; that, in fact, nothing ugly exists, or that, if it does exist, it can never appear to any one. And this seems an outrageous paradox. Nevertheless it is a truth, and an important truth. Nothing is ugly except in a qualified and relative sense ; a picture or a view which is described as ugly is never wholly and simply ugly, but is always a mixture of ugliness and beauty, and it is the presence of the beauty that alone makes the ugliness possible. Nor can such an object be dissected into beautiful parts and ugly parts. It is not that all ugliness is mitigated by streaks of beauty, for this is not necessarily the case ; it is rather that all ugliness consists of a beauty, which is actually felt as beautiful, but is in some way frustrated or spoilt. All ugliness is beauty spoilt, beauty uglified. In music, the ugliness of a wrong note depends on the rightness of the other notes ; this rightness is musical beauty, and the ugliness of the total effect depends on the destruction of a real and actual beauty by the intrusion of something alien to it, something which yet in itself is not ugly at all, for the wrong note would be right in another key. Ugliness is the destruction of beauty ; it presupposes a beauty to be destroyed ; and when it has completely destroyed this beauty it ceases to be ugliness and starts fair, so to speak, with a chance of achieving a new beauty of its own. When all sense of key has disappeared because all the notes are wrong notes, one may get the new beauty of keyless sound.

But further, all ugliness, so far as it does actually exist, is not the ugliness of an object imagined but the ugliness of an object not imagined : not imagined, that is, in the strict sense of the word. When a person engaged in thought makes a mistake, we say that he has not really thought ; we exhort him to think, and we take it as obvious that one cannot think anything out and at the same time think it falsely. In the same way, when some one imagines something ugly, he has not really imagined ; he has not 'imagined out' the object, but has been content with half-imagining it. Error is not the absence of thought, nor yet something that is possible when thought is wholly and truly present ; it is confused thinking, passing over from thinking this to thinking that without noticing the transition. So ugliness is not the absence of imagination, nor yet something that may happen when imagination in the full sense is present ; it is confused imagining, an imagining that slips over from one imagination to another without imagining out any one thing to the end.

Hence comes the idea that ugliness is a low degree of beauty, or that beauty is the perfection which, when missed in varying degrees, gives place to varying degrees of ugliness. But it is clear from what has been said that neither beauty, which is unity, nor ugliness, which is lack of unity, admits of degree. A low degree of beauty means a beauty which we can apprehend with a comparatively slight exertion of imaginative energy; such a beauty is a trivial, hackneyed, or vulgarized beauty, and these epithets describe it qualitatively.

Beauty is the unity or coherence of the imaginary object : ugliness its lack of unity, its incoherence. This is no new doctrine ; it is generally recognized that beauty is harmony, unity in diversity, symmetry, congruity, or the like. But such phrases are only generic, not specific ; for truth also, and utility, and goodness, may all be described in the same kind of language. That which distinguishes beauty from these is that it is not any unity, but an imaginative unity. This is a specific unity whose source is the unity of the act of imagination.

When we imagine, it does not matter what we imagine. There is no external necessity that can circumscribe the possible objects of imagination ; each act of imagination creates its object out of nothing and is indifferently free to create anything. But there is an internal necessity which imagination must obey. Whatever we imagine, we must imagine that, and not anything different. We may or may not imagine our hero as dying on the last page ; but if we do, we must not imagine anything inconsistent with this. We must 'imagine out' his death in all its implications ; we must imagine him in a world where a death of this particular kind is possible ; we must imagine that his life is such as to expose him to this death. Thus the whole story will be self-coherent ; it will be a unity in diversity, a harmony of its various parts. The mere act of imagination, by being itself, by being this act and not a different act, generates in its object that unity which is beauty. But it is clearly possible to imagine different and incompatible things and to waver between one act of imagination and another, to fail to make up one's mind whether one is imagining one version of a story or a different version ; and in that case the story falls to pieces, loses its unity, becomes confused and ugly.

The achievement of this unity, like the achievement of truth, may be the result of a happy accident or of a training which has become effortless. But the deliberate pursuit of it is the deliberate effort to imagine coherently ; and it is the presence of this effort that seems to distinguish art in the full sense of the word from dreaming. To dream is to imagine, but not to work at imagining ; when we dream, we are doing in a lazy and haphazard way the same thing which in creating a work of art we are doing with critical care and labour. Consequently our dreams now attain beauty, and now give an impression of jarring and idiotic ugliness, and this by no good or bad management on our own part. Yet, though we do not deliberately work at constructing our dreams, they are never entirely formless ; and their form is not the result of chance, but the fruit of those activities which we repress and control when we deliberately construct a work of art. Every deliberate activity has, as its negative side, the repression of another activity, which reasserts itself when our active control fails. A dangerous sport involves the repression of fear ; and when we fail to maintain the activity of climbing, fighting or the like, our fear rises up and threatens to overcome us. Hence the structure of dreams reveals under analysis the nature of the activities which in full-blown art are repressed ; and this is the principle which underlies the practice of psycho-analysis.

But to control our imagination by the deliberate attempt to ' imagine out ' an object cannot consist in selecting, out of a number of alternatives, something to be imagined. For in that case all the alternatives must be already present to the mind, that is, already imagined. In thinking something out, as Kepler thought out the paths of the planets, we imagine the alternatives

and then accept one and reject the rest ; but in imagination the
first stage does not exist. In making up a tune, we do not try
the various notes to see which to put next ; we imagine the whole
tune, and then, if we are dissatisfied with it, reimagine it afresh
with some change which in altering a single note alters the quality
of the whole. Hence the will to imagine is a will which does not
contemplate alternatives ; it is an ' immediate ' will, a will merely
to do what one is doing. And in this way art is the most primitive
practical activity, just as it is the most primitive theoretical
activity.

§ 6. *The Monadism of Art.*—In imagining, we do not contemplate the alternative possible imaginations. It follows that the
coherence or unity which is the goal of imagination is a coherence
of this individual imagination with itself, and not with any other.
So far as it is a successful piece of imagining considered in itself,
it is beautiful ; and this beauty is quite unaffected by the question
whether anybody else or I myself at another time have imagined
anything compatible or incompatible with it. In this, imagining
is sharply opposed to thinking. To imagine is to isolate the
object ; to think is to place it in a world of objects with which
it is continuous. The coherence of imagination is a merely
internal coherence ; the coherence of thought is an external
coherence, self-transcending as the other is self-contained. If
two plays are written about Julius Caesar, presenting incompatible
versions of his character, they may both be beautiful ; but if two
biographies of him are incompatible, they cannot both be true.

The self-transcendence of thought implies that there is in the
last resort only one object of thought, namely reality as a whole ;
within this one object every individual object of thought has its
place, conditions every other and is conditioned by them in its
turn. The unity of the real world does not cancel or make
illusory the plurality of its parts ; it is the unity not of an abstract
and indivisible unit but of a totality whose very being lies in the

diversity of its interrelated parts. Whenever we think of any single thing as real, we are assuming, consciously or unconsciously, the infinite context of reality as a whole ; and whenever we speak of reality as a whole we are focusing our thought upon some one part or feature of it, which is emphasized to the exclusion of the rest. Every perception, every judgement of science or history or philosophy, has this twofold aspect.

But there is nothing of this kind in the case of art. One work of art does not imply another ; in imagining one work of art we are not implicitly imagining all other works of art, we are ignoring them ; and to ignore an imaginary object is simply to condemn that object to non-existence so far as my world is concerned, for my world, as an imaginary world, only exists in my act of imagination. Hence to imagine one work of art is not to deny all others, for that which is denied must simultaneously be imagined ; it is simply not to imagine any other, and therefore the world of which, in that act, one is imaginatively aware is a world consisting of this one work of art and nothing else whatever.

Every work of art as such, as an object of imagination, is a world wholly self-contained, a complete universe which has nothing outside it. As soon as the existence of anything else is recognized simultaneously with its own, it no longer exists as a work of art at all, for it is no longer being imaginatively contemplated. This may be expressed by saying that every work of art is a monad, a windowless and self-contained world which mirrors the universe from its own unique point of view, and indeed is nothing but a vision or perspective of the universe, and of a universe which is just itself. Nothing can go into it or come out of it ; whatever is in it must have arisen from the creative act which constitutes it.

Nevertheless, if we look at works of art not from the aesthetic point of view but from the historical, we find that there is a plurality of them. The imaginative act as such can never be aware of anything but its own self-contained object ; but reflection upon this imaginative act reveals it as only one in a system of mutually exclusive or monadic works of art. The historical point of view reveals the existence of an indefinite plurality of these, and is able to detect relations between them : relations of succession, resemblance, dependence, and so forth. Whereas the aesthetic point of view is solely concerned with the appearance of the world as seen from this point, the historical point of view is concerned with the manner in which the observer has arrived at that particular aesthetic point of view. The problem of the genesis of a given work of art is a problem with which art as such has nothing to do ; the artist neither knows nor cares whether the work he is now creating is original or imitative, what suggested it, and so forth ; but the historian of art is concerned precisely with this problem of genesis. From this genetic point of view it becomes clear that any given work of art is based upon the entire previous experience of the artist ; not his artistic experience, but his whole experience ; and that it is, historically considered, an attempt to concentrate this whole experience into a single imaginative view of reality. What the artist sees as an absolutely unique creation, the historian sees as another attempt added to the long list of previous attempts to express the meaning of life in a symbolic form. Both the artist and the historian regard the work of art as expressive : but whereas the artist regards it as expressive simply of itself, the historian regards it as expressive of the experiences, now forgotten, which have paved the way for its creation.

To speak of looking at works of art from the aesthetic point of view and from the historical point of view does not imply that what is seen from these two points of view is the same thing. The work of art is seen as a work of art only from the aesthetic point of view : cease to look at it imaginatively, and it ceases to be a work of art : what you are now looking at is not a work of art at all but something different in kind, an historical fact, namely the fact that this particular aesthetic act has occurred. The reflective and historical knowledge that this act has occurred is a different act of consciousness from the act itself, and the objects of these two acts are no less different than the acts themselves.

It will be seen at a later stage of the argument that the aesthetic and reflective points of view are not the exclusive property of the artist and the historian or critic respectively: for, as we shall see, not only are the historian and critic at bottom the same, but the artist is only a conscious and deliberate artist because he is also a critic; and clearly, the critic can only be a critic because he is an artist first and foremost. Hence the monadism of art is a monadism which, establishing itself afresh in every aesthetic act, is broken down afresh by every act of historical or critical reflection: and all actual artistic work consists in the balancing of these two activities.

§ 7. *Art in its Specific Nature : Emotionally, as the Enjoyment of Beauty.*—Every activity is at once pleasant and painful: pleasant in so far as it succeeds in being or doing what it is trying to be or do, painful in so far as it fails. The pleasure and the pain can never be altogether separated; for the effort to do a thing is a mark of insufficient power or skill, and is therefore necessarily painful; where no effort is involved, the activity ceases to have any emotional colouring at all, and is therefore no longer pleasant. Failure and success are relative terms: when we fail, we succeed in doing something, even if it was not the thing we wanted to do: when we succeed, we do what we wanted to do, but that is no longer the thing we now want. Pleasure and pain are therefore two poles of an experience which is the emotional sense of our own activity; they are not distinct experiences, but a given activity may be called pleasant rather than painful so far as we feel ourselves overcoming its difficulties, painful rather than pleasant so far as we feel ourselves strained in the effort to do so,

Pleasure and pain, though in a sense they are the same things wherever they occur, have their own peculiar quality for every specific activity. These specific differences immediately distinguish the pleasure of one kind of experience from that of another, and they are as incapable of being described as of being interchanged. To explain how the pleasure of poetry differs from the pleasure of bathing is as impossible as to explain how red differs from blue. But the specific diversity of pleasures goes much further than this. There is an equally indescribable, and equally unmistakable, difference between the aesthetic pleasure of natural beauty and that of the beauty of art; between the beauty of a pattern and the beauty of a portrait, and so forth. These differences in themselves can only be felt; but they have grounds or conditions which can be described; and an attempt will be made to describe some of these in later chapters.

The presence of an emotional side is universal in all activity; but its presence is generally thought to be peculiarly necessary, and its function peculiarly central, in the case of art. No one would, except in joke, define justice as that which pleases the legal mind, or assert that the function of mathematical truth is to give pleasure to mathematicians; but people have seriously maintained that beauty is that which pleases in a certain way, or pleases a certain type of mind, or even, simply, pleases; and it is clear that hedonism, while no doubt just as unsatisfactory in the philosophy of art as in logic or ethics, is a great deal more plausible here than elsewhere.

The reason for this is that beauty is not a quality of objects apprehended by perception, nor yet a concept grasped by thought; it is an emotional colouring which transfuses the entire experience of the imagined object. In a previous section beauty has been defined as imaginative coherence. This coherence is qualitatively, as well as quantitatively, distinct from the coherence of an object of thought. Quantitatively, the coherence of imagination is the coherence of the object with itself, whereas the coherence of thought is not merely this but also a further coherence of the object with other objects as parts of a larger whole. But there is also a qualitative distinction. The coherence of the object of thought is apprehended intellectually or discursively as a system of relations between parts each of which can be thought of separately; the coherence of the object of imagination is intuitively felt as an incandescence, so to speak, of the whole. It is only under analysis that this incandescence or emotional colouring is found to consist in an immediate or intuitive awareness of relations between the parts of the object. What is felt as a peculiar thrill, indescribable but easily recognizable, at the point in the Waldstein Sonata which a small boy used to call the ' moon-rise ', turns out on analysis to be the contrast between the key of E major and that of C in which the sonata began; the thrill is the fusion of these two keys into a single indivisible experience in which each acquires its significance from the simultaneous awareness of the other.

This qualitative peculiarity of imaginative coherence, as a felt quality running through the whole rather than an articulated system of relations between its parts, results necessarily from its quantitative peculiarity. In order to follow out a system of relations in all its detail, one must be able to think first of one and then of another: to concentrate on one part at a time, and pass on to the next. When this is done, each part presents itself as the distinct object of a distinct act of thought; and because the whole world is implied in the thought of any given object, therefore, and in the same way, the whole object is implied in the thought of any of its parts. But to imagine a given object is not to imagine any other; and therefore to imagine any part of an object is not to imagine the rest. Hence, from the imaginative or aesthetic point of view, a work of art is not divisible into parts at all; that which appears to reflective analysis as a part is from the aesthetic point of view fused with the rest into an indivisible whole. The sonnet may be divided into lines and words, but what is divided is not that imaginative experience which is the sonnet regarded as a work of art, but something which may by reflection be shown to be a condition of that experience. This is why a work of art is always in danger of losing what painters call breadth through minute attention to detail; as soon as the artist really concentrates on a detail, the whole has vanished. Breadth, which means unity, can only be obtained when each detail is felt not as a part but as a modification of the whole.

The imaginative activity is therefore one in which the relation between theoretical, practical, and emotional elements is peculiarly close. It is impossible for a scientist to discover a truth without emotion; yet it is easy to distinguish the truth from the emotion of discovering it. But in the case of art this distinction cannot be made. Beauty is present to the mind simply in the form of an emotion. This emotion is bipolar; it is not merely pleasant, but pleasant and painful; and whereas those people who never go very deep into art regard it as a pleasant experience, but one whose pleasure is somewhat trivial and unimportant, those who exert their imaginative powers to the utmost find in that exertion not only a higher and more valuable pleasure but frequent and intense pain. This pain is caused not only by the spectacle of bad art, but equally, though in a different way, by all acute awareness of beauty; so much so that one constantly finds oneself afraid to go to a concert, to read a poem, to look at a very beautiful scene, not from fear of possible ugliness but from fear of too great beauty; and it is this fear that prompts the hatred and suspicion which a respectable mediocrity feels towards the highest art and the greatest splendours of nature.

The Forms of Beauty

§ 8. *The Forms of Beauty.*—The term beauty has hitherto been used in a general sense as a name for that quality of an object in virtue of which it satisfies the claims of the aesthetic spirit. But though this use of the word is legitimate, it requires both defence and modification. We are accustomed to think that some works of art aim not so much at beauty as at sublimity, pathos, humour, tragedy, and so forth. Sometimes we tend to distinguish these from beauty and to say that such and such a picture is sublime but not beautiful, such and such a woman pretty but not beautiful, and so forth ; in which case we generally regard beauty not as merely on a level with the rest but as a higher thing, and the thing which all works of art ought ideally to possess ; though people sometimes rebel against this view and regard it as no less monstrous to claim that all art should be beautiful than to claim that all art should be comic, thus implying that beauty is one only among a number of species of a genus, aesthetic excellence, for which we have no name. Sometimes, on the other hand, we do not distinguish sublimity, pathos, and the rest from beauty, but only from each other, regarding them as the species of beauty, the various forms into which it is differentiated.

These differences of view are perplexing, and our perplexity increases when we observe that there seem to be as many of these forms of beauty as one chooses to distinguish, and that the methods of defining and classifying them seem to be as arbitrary as their number. And hence it would seem a wholly desirable simplification of the philosophy of art to ignore them altogether ; to recognize one and only one form of aesthetic excellence, which may conveniently be called beauty, and to maintain that these forms of beauty are merely arbitrary ways of cutting up and sorting the infinite plurality of beautiful objects—a task whose motives are not aesthetic at all, but merely motives of con-

venience, as the arrangement of words in a dictionary is a question of convenience and not of philology.

But this proposed simplification, though certainly itself convenient, is not satisfying. No one thinks that there is any philological significance in the alphabetical arrangement of a dictionary, but every one has always thought that there is some aesthetic significance in the distinction between the sublime and the comic. And it is impossible to explain why a question of convenience in the sorting and cataloguing of works of art should ever have been confused with a question concerning their aesthetic quality. Certain predicates attached to works of art are intended and taken as implying a judgement on their aesthetic quality ; others are not. If we call a work of art sublime, or idyllic, or lyrical, or romantic, or graceful, we mean to call attention to something in the character of the work itself, and what we say about it amounts to praise or blame of the artist as such. On the other hand, if we call it a seascape or a villanelle or a fugue we are attaching to it a predicate with no aesthetic significance whatever, and are therefore neither praising it nor blaming it. Some words are used in both ways : thus to call something a tragedy may mean that it has a peculiar kind of aesthetic quality, or merely that it deals with a certain type of subject.

Distinctions of this kind reappear in other fields. For instance, we may attach to actions either predicates which indicate their moral quality or predicates which do not. It is perfectly legitimate to classify an act as an instance of knocking a man down or writing a cheque ; but nobody thinks that when we do so, we are in any sense pronouncing upon the moral quality of the act, and nobody would think it necessary for moral philosophy to enter into such classifications. But it would be absurd to seize upon this obvious truth as an excuse for banishing all conceptions from the field of moral philosophy except the one conception of the good, and for maintaining that moral philosophy need not consider distinctions like that between expediency and duty or law and conscience. In the same way, the philosophy of art must steer between the Scylla of attaching falsely aesthetic values to predicates which have no aesthetic intention, merely because they are predicated of works of art, and the Charybdis of denying the existence of distinctions within the one concept of beauty, swallowing up the diversities of the aesthetic spirit in its unity, and reducing itself to the repetition of an empty formula.

The double danger is perhaps due to an excessive confidence in the logic of classification. A genus divides into species in such a way that whatever is in the genus falls in one species and only one. Now if the sublime, the comic, and the rest are species of the beautiful, then every work of art is, first, beautiful, and, secondly, sublime or comic or what not. But sometimes we call a work of art both sublime and comic ; and sometimes we say—generally with a suggestion of dispraise—that something is sublime or comic or tragic but not beautiful. To explain the former case away by saying that *Hamlet* is not one work of art but a variety entertainment composed of tragic and comic fragments is to proclaim the bankruptcy of one's theory; to dismiss the latter as a mere freak of language is to confess one's inability to understand what the people who use this language mean.

The beautiful and its various forms are not related either as species of an unnamed genus, or as a genus, beauty, and its species. The highest beauty somehow contains within itself, as subordinate and contributory elements, both the sublime and the comic, and indeed all other forms of beauty ; so that these forms appear as parts of a whole, the whole being beauty. But where these elements fall apart, where we get one form in apparent isolation, we do not wholly fail of beauty : the one element constitutes a beauty in itself, but a beauty of a truncated and incomplete kind, beauty at a lower level of development. A good joke is beautiful in its way, and in its way completely beautiful ; yet it is only a joke, and this ' only ' marks an aesthetic shortcoming ; its beauty is of a limited and defective kind, so much so that we might hesitate even to call it beautiful at all, but might prefer to say that it was not beautiful, but only comic. But a joke skilfully set in a context of tragedy overcomes this defect. It does not become any funnier, but it becomes beautiful with the beauty of a complete and balanced work of art, a beauty to whose completeness it contributes something vital, and whose completeness, thus achieved, is reflected upon itself.

The forms of beauty, then, are not mutually exclusive forms ; indeed they are mutually implicative, and each gains, rather than loses, by fusion with the rest. To argue that sublimity, for instance, cannot be a distinguishable aesthetic predicate because every true work of art turns out on inspection to contain something of the sublime, is to confess oneself the victim of a logical blunder, and to discredit not the concept of sublimity, but the use one is making of the logic of genus and species ; it is like arguing that because this table is brown it cannot also be square, unless brownness and squareness are identical.

The following sections are an attempt to distinguish the forms of beauty and to give an account of their mutual implications ; but not to do this exhaustively. The parts of a whole cannot be exhaustively enumerated, because within these other parts can always be distinguished *ad infinitum*. All we shall do is to distinguish enough of these forms to exhibit the principle involved in the distinction ; while fully recognizing that a closer examination of our pattern at any point would reveal pattern within pattern.

§ 9. *The Sublime.*—It is generally said that the sublime has some special connexion with overwhelming power ; but what this connexion is, authorities are not agreed. If, as they sometimes seem to imply, a work of art is sublime when it depicts a very powerful thing, and if a natural object is sublime when,

in addition to being beautiful, it is also very powerful, then
sublimity is not an aesthetic predicate at all, for it marks not
a special kind of beauty but a special kind of situation in which
beauty may—or may not—be found. But this is not a just
account of the way in which the word sublimity is actually used.
A picture of an elephant, an express locomotive, a storm at sea,
or a great mountain, does not acquire a title to the name sublime
merely on account of the scale and power of its subject ; nor is
it true that the aesthetic feelings with which we regard such
powerful things are always and as a matter of course described as
sublime feelings. And on the other hand the word is often used
in cases where no such power is evident. These facts are generally
admitted, and the theory has been modified to meet them by
extending the notion of power first to ' moral ' power, which
would permit us to extend the notion of sublimity to the spectacle
of weakness and defeat heroically endured, and then to the consciousness of power elsewhere than in the object, as for instance
in ourselves or in God. But the real difficulty of the conception
lies not in adjusting the definition to the extent of the things
defined, but in determining what precisely is meant by power.

It is plain that physical force and bigness, and what is called
moral force, have nothing essential to do with sublimity. Any
object may be found sublime if approached from the right point
of view ; just as a beautiful object is not an object having a special
kind of shape or colour but an object which the beholder regards
imaginatively, so a sublime object is not one possessed in itself
of certain attributes but one which the beholder regards with
that peculiar modification of the imaginative attitude which
stands to sublimity as imagination in the absolute sense stands
to beauty. It is in our relation to the object, not in the object
considered apart from that relation, that the ground of sublimity
must be sought.

That power or force which makes an object sublime can only

be its power over us; and not any power, but a specifically aesthetic power, power to make us realize its beauty. Sublimity, therefore, is beauty which forces itself upon our mind, beauty which strikes us as it were against our will and in spite of ourselves, beauty which we accept passively and have not discovered, by a deliberate search for it, in the place where we should expect to find it. Some such feeling of passive acquiescence in a beauty that seems to sweep upon us and overwhelm us from without is never altogether absent from any aesthetic experience, and therefore all beauty has some tinge of sublimity; but the most striking cases of sublimity are those in which this unexpectedness is most marked. Such are cases where our mind has been preoccupied by cares other than aesthetic; where we have been obsessed by fear or desire, or where we have habitually regarded some object as merely useful or merely a nuisance. Thus a person who lives among mountains sees them rather as beautiful than as sublime; but a person who, climbing them in fatigue and in some fear, suddenly becomes conscious of their beauty, which so long as he is wholly absorbed in his climbing he cannot do, sees their beauty as sublimity. So the noise of a bombardment, the buildings of factories and engineering works, a distorted human face, and other things which are generally regarded either as positively ugly or as having no aesthetic character at all, reveal their beauty in the form of sublimity.

The sublime is the first and most elementary form of the beautiful. Sublimity is the mere revelation of beauty as beauty, the inrush of aesthetic experience. At the first moment of its enjoyment, in its absolute novelty, as an absolute creation, all beauty is sublime and nothing else. But conservation is only sustained creation, and that activity whose first fulguration is pure sublimity must continue to be freshly active at every point of its course; and hence all beauty is sustained by a spring of sublimity at its heart.

§ 10. *The Comic.*—But the experience of sublimity contains an element of illusion which makes it unstable. The power which is sublimity appears in that experience as belonging to an object which compels us in spite of ourselves to admire it ; the object seems to be active, we to be passive. But this is not really the case. The power which we attribute to the object is really our own ; it is our own aesthetic activity. The shock of sublimity is the shock of an uprush of imaginative energy within ourselves ; and the illusion consists in the fact that we do not feel this energy as our own. No doubt, it is an energy which we could not stifle if we would, for the act by which we would stifle it could only be another manifestation of it, and hence we are not able to choose whether we shall manifest it or not ; but this is not because the power in question is a power outside ourselves, but because it is ourselves.

The sublime object is therefore in something of a false position, or rather we by regarding it as sublime have put ourselves in a false position ; we are worshipping an idol whose divine attributes are only the magnified shadow of our own powers. Now this might be discovered reflectively by philosophical analysis ; but it may also be discovered intuitively by merely finding that the sublime object, when the first shock of its revelation is over, ceases to impress us as sublime. It is a familiar fact that the experience of sublimity is unstable, and that what we first find sublime we find on further acquaintance perhaps beautiful, perhaps merely pretentious ; and this change of attitude, experienced by the aesthetic consciousness and descriptively recorded by psychology, is explained by the conception of sublimity as the first form of beauty, the initiation of an act which, once initiated, must necessarily pass beyond its own starting-point. If then sublimity is the first approximation of the aesthetic experience towards the ideal of beauty, the second approximation must be the correction of the error involved in the first. This error was the ascription of power to the object and of passivity to the beholder; the correction of this must be the recognition that the object owes its sublimity to the observer's act; and the intuitive or non-philosophical form of this recognition will be a feeling of power on one's own part, correlative to a feeling that the object is not in itself the awe-inspiring thing we had fancied it. Where we had exalted the object and abased ourselves, we now exalt ourselves and abase the object.

This change of attitude is the proverbial step from the sublime to the ridiculous. To find an object ridiculous involves a certain contempt of it, just as to find an object sublime involves a certain awe of it; and laughter has sometimes been regarded as a symptom of contempt merely. This is too simple an account of the matter. No one likes being laughed at; but if nature had devised laughter as an instinctive expression of social criticism, she would have produced a very clumsy mechanism for her purpose. The theory of laughter belongs to the philosophy of art; the satisfaction which we find in it is an aesthetic satisfaction, and to this extent the comic is a form of the beautiful. But it is that form of the beautiful in which the aesthetic quality is felt to depend not on the object but on the subject; and therefore a ridiculous object is not necessarily a beautiful object, but may be, and in the cases where the element of ridicule appears in the purest form generally is, an object definitely felt as not beautiful. Hence the comic has often been regarded as a peculiar case of the ugly, an ugliness which does not outrage our aesthetic sensibilities but gives them scope for a peculiar kind of activity. Such a definition is sound as far as it goes, but it fails to account for the fact that we find many things amusing which are far from ugly; the fact that there is a friendly and sympathetic laughter as well as a hostile, a cynical, and a defiant.

The comic is the object of an aesthetic frame of mind which may be called the revolt or reaction against sublimity. The shock

with which we discover a beauty dies away : we become familiar
with the object, and familiarity breeds a feeling that the beauty
which we saw in it was our own work and not due to any real
power in the object. The object no longer overawes or impresses
us with its beauty, and this release from awe, uprush of positive
self-feeling, or, as Hobbes called it, ' sudden glory ', is what we
express by laughter. The pricked bubble of sublimity collapses
into ridicule ; and we never in fact laugh without the feeling
that something is breaking up, that some tension is relaxed, that
some mountain's labour has brought forth a mouse, that something has failed to justify its pretensions. But a mere collapse
or disappointment is not comic ; it must be an aesthetic collapse,
a collapse of the sublime, a collapse of something that has impressed
us not just anyhow, but aesthetically. And yet to be impressed
by anything—an opinionated man who infects us with the belief
in his own knowledge ; a dangerous sea-crossing ; an alarm of
fire ; an angry bull—has an aesthetic side in which we find that
thing sublime ; and therefore when the thing in question turns
out not to be formidable, the feeling of sublimity is dissipated in
laughter. Hence we tend to laugh at any escape from danger or
anxiety ; the child laughs on getting out of school, and we all
have an unregenerate tendency to laugh when we see another
overtaken by a misfortune which we have ourselves escaped. This
is a crude and barbarous laughter because it is based on forgetting
that we too are subject to the same misfortunes, and that school
will begin again ; and these reflexions are apt to kill our mirth.
But they do not kill it outright. There is a higher type of laughter
which remembers our own frailty, faces our own perils, and yet
refuses to be impressed by them ; which finds in our own weakness
a source of mirth not because it is weakness but because we can
rise above it. This type of laughter selects for its object just
those things of which we are afraid, such as sex, death, or God.
Here it is not the release from fear that gives rise to laughter,

but the triumph over a fear of which we are still conscious ; we will not allow ourselves to be overcome by pain and misfortune and the sense of our own littleness and impotence, and therefore we face pain with a smile and make a joke of our own feebleness. This laughter is free from barbarity, and tinged with a certain heroism ; but it is essentially an act of defiance, and hence it degenerates into cynicism, blasphemy, and obscenity ; we are laughing at ourselves, for to blaspheme is to mock not God but our own religious impulses ; and this involves despising ourselves and our common human nature. But this self-degradation, this despising of ourselves in order to assert our own superiority over the self we despise, is a self-contradictory attitude, and the laughter which expresses it is a jarring and tuneless mirth. After all, contemner and contemned are one ; and the reassertion of this unity is the act by which the defiant laughter of cynicism is mellowed into humour.

The humorous frame of mind is that in which we laugh at a weakness which we no longer feel as contemptible. Rather, we sympathize with it and do not wish it otherwise, but love it for what it is. There is still a sense of our own superiority to the object, a sense of our strength as contrasted with its weakness : without that, there would be no amusement. But this sense of superiority is no longer contemptuous. We have recovered from the shock of realizing that the object is a weak thing, and have resigned ourselves to the certainty that it is so ; and therefore humour has in it a note of melancholy, of pessimism, and even at times of despair. Humour is the highest form of laughter, and at the same time it is comedy passing over into tragedy.

§ 11. *The Beautiful.*—The sublime and the comic have been taken in the preceding sections as the first and second forms of the beautiful. Each is beautiful, but in an incomplete and one-sided way. In each case there is a discord between the sub-ject and the object which mars the perfection of the aesthetic enjoyment: either the one or the other is unworthy of its correlative, and the result is a lack of balance, an imperfection in the harmony which here, as in every activity, must ideally subsist between subject and object. The disillusionment of laughter is the end of an illusion, but it is itself another illusion, equal and opposite. To overcome both illusions would be to attain the stability in which alone the mind can present to itself a truly beautiful object. But one illusion has already been overcome; and it only remains to overcome the other.

The negative illusion of ridicule has no function except as a counterblast to the positive illusion of sublimity: and therefore, when it has done its work, it exhausts itself for very lack of work to do. It is only in the actual collapse of sublimity that ridicule can exist; when the sublimity has effectively collapsed, the ridicule has consumed its fuel and burnt itself out. A person who has thoroughly eradicated from his mind that false awe of an object which makes him see it as sublime no longer laughs at it.

The cancelling-out of these opposites brings us back in a sense to our starting-point. But it is not a question of mathematics, in which 1 added to − 1 makes 0, but of actual experience, in which a movement and a counter-movement leave us enriched by something through which we have lived, and enable us, or rather compel us, to take up a new attitude towards the same starting-point. Once more, we find ourselves impressed by the sublimity of the object; but now we anticipate the collapse of this sublimity into ridicule; we feel the collapse immanent within the sublimity, and so experience both at once instead of trying to maintain the one by itself till the other forces itself upon us in a revulsion of feeling. Had they been mere contradictories this would have been impossible; had each been nothing but the negation of the other, no synthesis could have been even attempted. But they have this in common, that each is the apprehension of an object which is in some sense beautiful ; and what cancels out is not their whole nature but only the complementary illusions which prevented each from being the full apprehension of a fully beautiful object. The synthesis of the sublime and the comic therefore gives us the beautiful in the full sense of the word.

The relation of the sublime and the comic to the beautiful is not exactly that of parts to a whole, just as it is not exactly that of species to a genus, though it resembles both these relations. In their isolation each is not a mutilated portion of beauty but a beauty, though an inferior and disturbed beauty ; whereas in the relation of whole and part, if all the parts are not present the whole is not present even in a modified degree. And in their synthesis each does not so much supplement the other as negate the other ; each loses its peculiar character, and the two thus sink their difference in what is now an identity ; whereas the parts of a whole are merely juxtaposed externally, each remaining wholly itself in order to make up what the other lacks. Thus in true beauty there is always present not so much sublimity itself as a transmuted form of sublimity ; the mind is not so much overwhelmed with the shock of an unexpected glory as touched to a calm solemnity, a hush in which it hears the voice of the authentic divinity. And there is also present not so much a frankly comic element as an element of sublimated comedy, laughter softened into that smile with which we all naturally contemplate beauty.

Between these two poles of sublimity and comedy lies the whole of that experience which is the contemplation of perfect beauty. When this experience is attained, but attained with a certain lack of clearness and fixity, the mind seems to oscillate between the two poles, on the point of lapsing now into the sublime and now into the comic, but always reacting in time against the threatened obsession and passing over to the opposite pole.

Very great works of art are produced by this oscillation ; the comic sculptures that incrust a medieval cathedral and the comic scenes that punctuate Elizabethan tragedy are marks not of a frivolity which is incapable of the high seriousness of sublime art, but of a mental balance which will not fall into the pompous pretentiousness of the unrelieved sublime or the cynical triviality of the purely comic, but displays the security of its grasp on true beauty by repeatedly touching first one and then the other of its limits. And a balance of the same kind is achieved when we laugh at a sublime work of art merely because it is sublime and not comic. Seriousness itself is funny because the mind of the beholder, in order to retain its own aesthetic balance, imports into its contemplation of a sublime object just that element of comedy which the object lacks ; and thus preserves itself from being engulfed in its sublimity. In this sense, and in this sense only, the ' sense of humour ' is symptomatic of a ' sense of proportion ', and the man who laughs shows himself a healthy and well-balanced man.

But this compensatory transition from one pole to the other, even in its highest form, where the artist himself in his own single person vibrates between the two poles, is an imperfect enjoyment of the beautiful ; it is rather a protest against two false ideals than an embodiment of the true. Hence there is felt to be a certain discord between the solemnity of the cathedral's structure and the ribaldry of its ornament ; and the ' comic relief ' of the old drama is felt by all critics to demand explanation. In such an oscillation between the two poles, the two remain separate ; their difference is still emphasized, and the single experience which was to be born of their union remains an unfulfilled promise. The highest art of all no longer vibrates in this way ; instead of leaping from one extreme to the other, it has come to rest in the centre.

The mark of this repose is a feeling which can best, perhaps, be described as one of intimacy with the object. The sublime and the comic are alike in this, that the object is held off at arm's length, looked up to in the one case, looked down upon in the other. The mind, in both cases alike, feels itself incommensurate with its object; the power which generates the aesthetic experience is felt as flowing either from object to subject, exciting beauty in a mind incapable of creating it for itself, or from subject to object, conferring beauty on something which in itself does not possess it. The question has sometimes been raised, whether beauty is 'objective' or 'subjective', by which is meant, whether it belongs to the object and is by it imposed on the mind by brute force, or whether it belongs to the mind and is by it imposed on the object irrespective of the object's own nature. The only meaning so strange a question can have, is whether the sublime or the comic is the true and only form of the beautiful. For real beauty is neither 'objective' nor 'subjective' in any sense that excludes the other. It is an experience in which the mind finds itself in the object, the mind rising to the level of the object and the object being, as it were, preadapted to evoke the fullest expression of the mind's powers. The experience of beauty is an experience of utter union with the object; every barrier is broken down, and the beholder feels that his own soul is living in the object, and that the object is unfolding its life in his own heart. Hence arises that absence of constraint, that profound sense of contentment and well-being, that characterizes the experience of real beauty. We feel that it is 'good for us to be here'; we are at home, we belong to our world and our world belongs to us.

But that is a merely psychological description of the experience. The feeling which we thus describe has a ground, and this ground can be made explicit by reflexion on the feeling. The aesthetic activity is the activity of imagination; and imagination creates its own object. Now the experience of sublimity is an act of imagination, and therefore creative of its own object; but in this experience itself we feel as if the object were evoking the act.

We are—always in terms of feeling, not in terms of philosophical theorizing—precisely inverting the true position, and erecting into a creator the object which in that very act we have created. Hence the experience of sublimity is an illusion not in the sense that it is a false philosophical theory, but in the sense that it is a feeling whose implications, when we reflect on them, are found to contain a false philosophical theory. This implicit error is implicitly corrected by the transition from the sublime to the comic, but only partly corrected. Again in terms of feeling, to ridicule an object is to regard its sublimity as imaginary, but to regard it, as a thing in itself, as not imaginary. We have stripped the object of its aesthetic quality, and left it naked and contemptible. But this stripped object is in point of fact still an aesthetic object, and therefore an object of imagination : it is an object which we have first created and then degraded, and at which therefore we have no right to laugh. We began by making ourselves an idol and worshipping it ; we go on, when our prayers are unanswered, to flog it ; the one attitude is as unreasonable as the other. To recover from both forms of unreason is to remember that the idol was made by ourselves to be the expression of our own thought ; and the intuitive awareness of this is the feeling of intimacy between our mind and the object which is simply our mind made visible to itself.

This does not imply that the only person who can truly enjoy the beauty of anything is the philosopher who knows that the object is the creature of his own imagination. To enjoy beauty is an imaginative act, not a reflective ; and the object of imagination cannot possibly become an object to philosophical thought. The imaginary can only be imagined : if we are to philosophize, we must philosophize not about the imaginary but about the real, not about the object of aesthetic experience but about the act that generates that object. But the enjoyment of beauty, as distinct from sublimity, does presuppose something beside the pure act of imagination : it presupposes the ability to learn from experience, to react differently to a given situation because a similar situation has developed in a particular way in the past.

3

The Beauty of Nature

§ 12. *The Imaginary Object and the Real Object.*—It has already been shown (§ 3) that to call an object imaginary is to express one's indifference as to whether it is real or not. If this is so, and if to imagine an object is to find it beautiful, there is no difficulty in the fact that we find real objects, whether natural objects or works of art, beautiful ; for it is just as possible to look imaginatively at these as it is to look imaginatively at objects which exist solely in our own imagination. It is therefore perfectly indifferent, as regards the beauty of an object, whether it is imaginary in the narrower sense of the word or real, and, if real, whether it is a natural object or a work of art. Of these distinctions the aesthetic activity ought to take no cognizance ; they belong to the region of reflective thought, not to the region of art. The artist, as artist, ought to look upon these different types of object with precisely the same feelings, and leave it to the philosopher to discriminate between them.

This is the position which would seem to follow necessarily from the general conception of art as imagination. That there is a certain amount of truth in it is undeniable. It is true that an object, whatever else may be said about it, is only beautiful to a person who looks at it imaginatively, and that the kind of beauty which he finds there depends on the intensity and character of his own imaginative activity. It is also true that the aesthetic act is not an act of perception and therefore does not and cannot either assert or deny the reality of its object, and is still less able

to assert that its object has come into existence in one kind of way
or in another.

But the fact remains that all artists are in the habit of distinguishing natural from artistic beauty, not as one and the same
thing found in objects between which philosophical reflection is
forced to distinguish, but as two things which are aesthetically
distinguishable. Just as it does not take a physicist to decide that
something is sublime, so it does not take a philosopher to decide
that something has that peculiar kind of beauty which is called
natural beauty. The force of the sublime is not physical energy
but aesthetic impressiveness; and in the same way the distinction between natural beauty and artistic beauty is not a metaphysical distinction, irrelevant to the artist as such, but a distinction
between two kinds of aesthetic experience. Both the natural
object and the work of art present themselves to the artist himself
as real and not merely imaginary : their reality enters into his
aesthetic experience as a constituent element, giving it a quality
of its own, and their different origin further differentiates this
quality.

But before discussing the distinction between natural and
artistic beauty it is necessary to raise the question why the purely
imaginative activity of art should ever come to regard its object
as real : that is, as independent of its own imaginative act. The
paradox lies in the fact that whereas imagination is by definition
unconcerned with the reality of its object, it includes one particular type of experience in which it regards its object as essentially
real ; in which that very distinction which lies outside the com-
petence of imagination appears somehow within imagination
itself, not in the form of an assertion—for imagination can never
assert—but in the form of a feeling which colours the quality of
the imaginative act.

The principle by appeal to which this paradox can be explained
is one which made its first appearance at the close of the last

section. It was there pointed out that the transition from the antithesis of the sublime and the comic to the beautiful could only be effected by a mind possessed of the capacity to learn from experience. A new and unique aesthetic experience was thus generated by a principle which was not itself aesthetic : for there is only one aesthetic principle, namely imagination : and yet the attitude of imagination to its own object is affected by this non-aesthetic principle. But the mere capacity to learn by experience is not the only non-aesthetic principle which may introduce a new quality into the aesthetic experience itself.

§ 13. *Inspiration.*—It may be doubted whether we ever imagine without also thinking. In most cases of dreaming, the objects of our dream-consciousness are merely imaginary ; but in point of fact we do in dreams make a distinction between reality and unreality, though as a rule we make it wrongly, and take for real what is only imaginary. In our waking imaginations we sometimes know that we are only imagining, and sometimes wrongly think that we are not. But there seems to be no case in which we make no judgement whatever as to whether we are imagining or not, in other words, whether the immediate object of our consciousness is a merely imaginary object or a real object ; and in many cases it is certainly true that when we are engaged in the aesthetic activity we know that we are so engaged. Indeed this must be so in all deliberately-controlled imagining, in all that we generally call art ; for the will to imagine implies the consciousness that we are imagining.

The artist, then, is always doing two things : imagining and knowing that he is imagining. His mind is as it were a twofold mind and has before it a twofold object : as imagining, he has before him the imagined object ; as thinking, he has before him his own act of imagining that object. He knows, and without this he could not be an artist, that he is aesthetically active ; but he does not understand the relation between this activity and the other activities which go to make up his nature, for he is not a philosopher. He thinks of himself as imagining but he does not think of himself as thinking; yet he is thinking, and so far his self-knowledge is an incomplete and misleading self-knowledge. The artist, as artist, imagines: as thinker, he watches himself imagining and by this watching makes it possible to concentrate himself on the task of imagining. The thinking self controls the imagining self and makes the difference between a random dreaming and the deliberate imagination of art. Yet though the thinking self controls the imagining self, the artist does not know that this is so; for he is only conscious that he is imagining, not that he is thinking; and therefore he knows that something is controlling his imaginative activity—something other than that activity itself—but does not know that this something is his own thought.

The consciousness that one's imagination is controlled by some power other than itself must be distinguished from the quite different feeling of passivity which characterizes the experience of the sublime. In contemplating natural beauty, we feel our faculties as adequate to apprehend the object, and the object as adequate to satisfy the demands of our faculties. The power which controls the imagination is felt to be, as it really is, a spiritual activity transcending the imagination but somehow akin to it: and in so far as the artist thinks of himself as all imagination, he thinks of this power as a spiritual activity transcending his own personality, a power which inspires him to imaginations which his own strength could never achieve. Of this inspiring power he feels himself to be the passive mouthpiece.

The inspiring power whose presence is felt by the aesthetic consciousness is in some sense a god; and therefore this feeling of inspiration might be thought a religious rather than an aesthetic feeling, or at least a point of transition from art to religion. But this would be an error. Religion begins when the mysterious powers which work upon human life are identified and named;

that is to say, when the centre of interest is no longer the effect produced by a force but that force itself. To feel oneself inspired, *pati deum*, is not religion but the raw material of religion ; the religious consciousness is one which has overcome this sheer passivity and has dared to inquire what the force that has possessed it is. Religion does not merely ' suffer ' God, it ' walks with ' God, holds some kind of communion with him, knows his name. And the aesthetic consciousness has no name for the power which inspires it ; it has a name only for the experience of being possessed by this power.

§ 14. *Nature.*—The belief that one is inspired takes its rise not in the pure act of imagination but in the thought by which one is conscious of oneself as imagining. It might be inferred that this belief could not, as it were, get inside the imagination and colour its activity, but would remain a thing of the intellect, an error—so far as it is an error—which, as thinkers, we make about our aesthetic experience, but which for that very reason cannot affect this experience itself. This would imply that imagination and thought are so far independent of one another that we can think what we please and leave the course of our imaginations unaltered. But every act of imagination is an imaginative reflection or resultant of the man's whole experience, and this experience includes his own thought about his own imaginative activity. If, in so far as he thinks, he recognizes that his imagination is controlled by an activity higher than itself, this recognition must leave its mark on his imagination in the form of a feeling of ' givenness ' which characterizes its awareness of its object.

Thus the feeling of ' givenness ' which at first sight seems to contradict the very definition of imagination is really a consequence of that definition ; and to suppose that imagination ought to imply an awareness of the object's character as imaginary is to confuse imagination with the philosophical understanding of imagination. It is just because art is art and not philosophy that the artist, whose business is to imagine and not to understand, feels his object as something independent of his imagining it.

The term nature, in whatever context it is used, bears a negative sense. It always indicates a limit of our own activity. Human nature is that which we cannot alter by moral or legislative effort; the forces of nature are those forces which we can only control by obeying them; natural laws and natural rights are those which exist whether human beings recognize them or not. The nature of anything is that which we must accept as an absolute datum; but this datum is correlative to an activity of our own. A starting-point has meaning only with reference to something that starts there : to say that we cannot alter the nature of a thing implies that there is something about it which we can and do alter. Therefore the idea of nature arises as the negative counter-part of the idea of activity, and every kind of activity has its counterpart in a distinct kind of nature. Thus nature in the aesthetic sense is that which we find ourselves under the necessity of imagining, as the starting-point or datum for any further act of imagining which feels itself to be a free act. But as, in per-ceiving, we feel everything that we perceive to be a natural object, and as, in thinking, the scientist feels every object of his thought to be a part of nature, so, in imagining, the artist feels every object of his imagination to be nature. In all these cases alike the cognitive activity feels its object to be independent of it and set over against it as a limit to its own freedom ; though in all these cases the question may be raised by philosophy, whether this feeling is not in some sense an illusion, and whether the object may not in reality be in some sense constituted by the very act which apprehends it.

That this is so in the case of imagination has already been shown. And therefore the feeling of givenness would appear, in this case at least, to be an illusion. But even if it is an illusion, it is a genuine feeling, one which actually enters into the imaginative experience and must be accepted for a fact by any account of that experience. Moreover it has been shown in the foregoing analysis to be a necessary fact, a feature which the imaginative activity is bound to develop. If then it is an illusion, it is a necessary illusion; and that is a way of saying that it is not altogether an illusion. In general, this sense of givenness is the finite mind awareness of its own finitude. A mind that was wholly finite could not be aware that it was finite; where finitude is known it is transcended. But where it is not explicitly or philosophically known but merely felt as the emotional background of an experience, it is not explicitly transcended; there is only a pledge that it can be transcended.

Hence the feeling of givenness in virtue of which the object of imagination is felt as real, as nature, is, properly considered, not an illusion at all, but the imaginative awareness of a profound truth. The artist, in virtue of this feeling, is aware that he is not the idle singer of an empty day, a teller of tales whose only justification is that they are good tales. On the surface, his work is a mere play of fancies; but behind this surface it is quick with a hidden truth, a meaning that goes far beyond what is explicitly said. The artist does not know this meaning; it is for him a mystery hidden behind the imagery that expresses it, a spirit at once revealed and concealed by the visible garment that it wears: but he feels its presence, and this feeling is the sense of inspiration; he traces the pattern in the garment, and this garment is nature.

All this the artist feels as an integral part of his aesthetic experience. He does not, so far as he is an artist, think it out philosophically; he does not even state it as a religious creed. It is present to him simply in the form of a peculiar emotional colouring in the object of his imagination. This emotional colouring would not be experienced at all unless the artist was capable of thinking as well as of imagining. If there could be a mind purely imaginative and devoid of all intellectual faculties, such a mind would be an artist, but its artistic experience would be altogether innocent of the feeling that its object was no mere fiction but a symbol of truth. But though these feelings have their source in thought, they are, as feelings, part and parcel of the aesthetic experience ; and necessarily so, because the imagina‑ tive faculty and the intellectual cannot in fact exist separately.

§ 15. *The Beauty of Nature.*—Because nature is a negative term, it always presupposes its corresponding positive. Nature in the aesthetic sense presupposes the aesthetic activity, and is the negation of this activity as felt by the activity itself. To call an object nature is to express the feeling that it is not in any sense the fruit of our own activity. Hence all beauty is natural beauty so far as it belongs to an object of which we feel ourselves not to be the makers. Whether we are really its makers or not is beside the point ; the question is simply what in the actual aesthetic experience we feel to be the relation between ourselves and the object. All beauty is natural beauty if and when we feel thus passively towards it. The object and our awareness of it are felt to be in perfect harmony with each other; but within this har‑ mony there is a distinction between feeling that the object is presented to the aesthetic activity, and feeling that the aesthetic activity, whether in myself or another, has created the object ; this is the distinction between the enjoyment of natural beauty and the enjoyment of the beauty of art.

The enjoyment of natural beauty is imagination unaware of its own creativity. When imagination discovers its own power of creating objects for itself, it feels itself as art in the fullest sense of the word, and its objects as works of art. Before this discovery, it feels itself as passively contemplating a ready-made nature. But the discovery is not a philosophical conception, it is a dis‑ covery made empirically, and therefore recognized in certain cases and not extended to other cases. Hence the distinction between the tang of two different feelings, the feeling of aesthetic receptivity and the feeling of aesthetic creativity, tends to be misinterpreted as a distinction between two species of beautiful objects. The result of such a misinterpretation is the attempt to classify beauties by dividing them into the two mutually-exclusive groups of natural and artistic; and the failure of any such attempt soon becomes evident. It is absurd to ask whether a given object, considered in itself and out of all relation to the imaginative act which apprehends it, is an instance of natural or artistic beauty; and no less absurd to assume, as any such classification must assume, that we take up the same imaginative attitude towards all objects which can be placed in the same class.

Nature is the antithesis not of my private or personal activity but of activity as such; and therefore that object is felt as nature which is felt as the limit or negation of the apprehending activity in general. In order to be aware of any beauty as natural beauty, I must be aware of myself as man; and then the beauty of nature will present itself as the beauty of the non-human world. So far as I am aware of myself, not merely as man in the abstract, but as man in a special aspect, nature will mean to me not the bare negation of humanity but the negation of this special aspect of humanity. Hence natural beauty presents itself in different forms correlative to the aspect of his own life which most deeply affects the observer's consciousness. Some of these will be considered in the following section.

All these forms have certain common characteristics. Nature is sometimes called the art of God; and the phrase admirably describes the actual experience, though it is couched in religious language which that experience would not itself naturally use. It implies what in that experience we always feel, that nature is impeccable. Nothing in nature is ugly; when we deny that a natural object is beautiful we are reflecting not upon it but upon ourselves. As such, every natural object is equally beautiful; God takes as much pleasure in the turbot and the hippopotamus as in the nightingale and the lion; his handiwork is a sufficient guarantee of perfection, and if we fail to see that perfection the fault is our own. This follows necessarily from the feeling of passivity: that feeling implies that beauty is everywhere around us in endless profusion, and that all we have to do is to accept what is given us. Natural beauty has no opposite: it is either seen or not seen. This gives it a peculiar quality of immediacy or spontaneity. It is something for which no one has worked, something that has come absolutely and exquisitely right by no effort, but by a pure act of divine grace. The lilies take no trouble over their clothes, and for that very reason their clothes are perfect. The mountain is beautiful because no one has built it, the forest because no one has planted it, the snowflake because no silversmith has touched it with hammer and file; the effortless immediacy of nature is in every case not something accidental to its beauty but the very heart of its beauty. The primrose of the rock is not both beautiful and not in a rock-garden; its not being in a rock-garden is the beauty of it. If art could so exactly reproduce a natural object that the eye could not detect the imposture, the reproduction, as soon as it was known to be a reproduction, would lose just that peculiar beauty which its natural archetype would possess. And in the same way nature is spoilt by adorning it; to gild the lily, to pinch and tattoo the human body, to plant a wild landscape with garden flowers, is to destroy the natural beauty of the object by interfering with this spontaneity. The same thing happens if the object is disturbed with no intention of adorning it, but either with another motive or in absence of mind: a railway or a quarry destroys the beauty of a mountain not by suggesting thoughts of utility but simply by cutting up the spontaneous flow of its lines; our joy in the beauty of a red toadstool is turned to disgust when we find the toadstool to be a Victoria plum dropped by a passer-by, not because we dislike plums or passers-by but because we had been enjoying the spontaneity of what we took to be nature's colour-scheme.

Natural beauty is thus beauty in its immediacy, a beauty whose special quality is its freedom from effort, from the attempt to realize something unrealized. There is the same difference between this effortless perfection and the result of artistic labour that there is between the goodness of a person who seems to do right by instinct, and that of one who does right by struggling with his temptations. Nature's song is the song of innocence : art's the song of experience.

§ 16. *The Forms of Natural Beauty.*—No aesthetic purpose would be served by a classification of natural beauties. The games of ' animal, vegetable, or mineral ', and ' earth, air, fire, and water ' have no place in the philosophy of art. But though an attempt to enumerate the various classes of object in which natural beauty may be found is of necessity both unsuccessful and unprofitable, there is within natural beauty a distinction of a different kind ; a distinction not between objects but between aesthetic points of view. Natural beauty in general is the beauty of an object which is felt to be the negation of the activity which contemplates it. According as man's self-consciousness undergoes any modification, that which he feels as his own opposite must undergo a parallel modification. In so far as he feels himself merely as man, nature will mean to him that which is not human. When he feels himself not merely as man but as civilized man, nature will be extended so as to include not only the non-human world but the world of human life in its uncivilized state ; and the definition of ' uncivilized ' will vary with the definition of ' civilized '. When he feels himself to be an artist, nature will be further extended to include even human life at his own level of civilization, so far as it is not inspired by consciously aesthetic motives. Thus, man conscious of himself as man finds natural beauty in the sea and the wind and the stars; man conscious of himself as civilized finds the same type of beauty in primitive human societies and their products : man conscious of himself as an artist finds the same type of beauty in machinery and other utilitarian products of civilization. The type of beauty involved in all these three cases is the same : it is the beauty of contrast between the spectator and his object, the beauty of that which is beautiful because it was not designed to be beautiful : in a word, the immediate beauty of nature. But the three cases represent three very different points of view. The taste which craves an object utterly remote from man is offended by the evidences of even the most primitive human activity ; it regards its object as desecrated if the landscape contains a single human figure, the seascape a single sail. The second frame of mind finds nothing incongruous in a nature modified by man, so long as the human influences are relatively primitive : the cottage, the tilled land, the old-fashioned town, fit into the beauty of nature without a jar, and for this frame of mind there is on the one hand something bleak and unsatisfying about the savagery of the purely natural world, while on the other it is offended by the railway, the factory, the steamship, and similar marks of industry. The third frame of mind is as dissatisfied with the spectacle of primitive man as the second is with untouched nature ; it regards the picturesque town and the rural countryside as insipid, and takes the same delight in the clean design of an express locomotive or a heavy gun that the first frame of mind takes in the modelling of a mountain and the articulation of a tree. Of these three attitudes, the first is the presupposition and basis of the others ; it is perpetuated in the second, because the enjoyment of scenery as such is in this second frame of mind not negated but regarded as by itself unsatisfying and in need of a supplement ; and it is still present in the third, because the beauty of utilitarian inventions is felt to depend upon the principle of conquering natural forces by obeying

them. These three phases of natural beauty must now be considered in turn.

(*a*) The first and most primitive is the beauty of pure nature.
Pure nature, or nature as such, is defined by contrast with man
as such. Man, conscious of his own activity, finds himself con-
fronted by a world which is not the fruit of that activity, and the
feeling of this givenness, this remoteness from his own interference, constitutes the special character of natural beauty in
this sense. The sun and moon and stars, the mountain and the
forest, the flowers and animals, the birds and fishes, the sea and
the river, the clouds and wind and rain, all have this beauty of
wildness. This feeling is not the fruit of a sophisticated civilization, except in the sense that to be self-conscious is already to be
sophisticated. It is not because the world is too much with us
that we turn to the beauty of wild things; unless indeed the
world simply means ourselves. The primitive savage feels this
beauty no less keenly than the town-dweller; primitive literature
is no less full of its echoes than the literature of an industrial age;
and the nature-worship which is especially characteristic of
uncivilized races represents a religious development of precisely
this feeling for the aesthetic power of wild nature. To people
the desert with naiads and oreads, spirits of the cloud and the
lightning, gods of vegetable growth and stellar movement, is to
betray the universality and depth of the feeling for pure natural
beauty.

This feeling is dissipated by finding traces of human action in
the natural object. When the wild is tamed, the beauty of its
wildness disappears; and hence the advance of human power
over nature always tends to restrict the scope and opportunities
of this frame of mind. As the desert is cultivated, as the river
is bridged and diked, as the mountain is quarried for stone and
the forest felled for timber, they cease to evoke the response
which was due to their defiance of human control; and since

these changes result necessarily from man's self-consciousness, the same gift which is the source of his enjoyment of their beauty is the source of his progressive destruction of that enjoyment. But there are always things which preserve their wildness; man cannot leave his mark upon the stars, and however he may defile the wind with smoke and the sea with oil, their own elemental energy, like the energy of vegetable growth, breaks in upon him unimpaired. There is still, and there must always be, an infinite field for the enjoyment of pure natural beauty.

But as man becomes more reflective and learns to see more in himself, pure nature ceases to satisfy him. The savage possibly enjoys it more than the civilized man; certainly among ourselves it is the young and the less reflective that find wild nature most lastingly satisfying. Not that any of us lose our joy in it; but as our own self-consciousness becomes deeper we tend to supplement it by additions and modifications which would have offended us at an earlier stage of our development, but which we now feel as enriching instead of destroying nature.

(*b*) These additions are based upon the principle that nature, to be beautiful, need no longer be wholly untouched by man; and that human interference, so far from impairing its beauty, may in certain circumstances even enhance it. To the eye which delights in pure natural beauty, the wild flower is delightful because it is in its right place; it fits into its surroundings, it has grown inevitably out of the influences of soil and climate, and this inevitability, though we may know nothing of geology and botany, is actually felt as an organic unity between the flower and the country in which it grows. But this very same unity may be felt in the case of human products. The cottage, built of oak beams or of bricks or of stone, seems to express the character of the soil on which it stands, and is beautiful not because it is built in one material rather than another, but because it is built in the material of which the landscape itself is built. The footpath across the moor adds to the beauty of the moor because it records the fashion in which men have picked their way across the country, and therefore subtly emphasizes the modelling and texture of that country. The arable lands and the meadows bring into relief, by their respective character, the varying qualities of the soil, no less than does the natural vegetation. Even the people, after living for generations in contact with nature, seem infected with the flavour of nature; they walk like shepherds, their eyes are the eyes of hillmen, their speech has modelled itself upon their occupations as their occupations have modelled themselves upon the land.

Even apart from the ways in which this human life has grafted itself upon nature and acquired something of nature's quality, it is felt to be in its own right a possessor of natural beauty. The manners and customs of such a society seem a kind of natural law, by contrast with the fashions of a sophisticated society; for they are the direct and unreflective expression of an immemorial tradition, which the individual is no more free to disregard than the individual rose is free to disregard the compulsion which makes it a rose. We take a peculiar pleasure in the spectacle of this life, its daily routine, its ceremonial of feast and holiday; a pleasure which is based on the feeling that there is here no conscious choice, no explicit question of whether a given act shall or shall not be done, a given costume worn or not worn. Thus we enjoy a Provençal carnival not because, considered as a work of art, it is above criticism, but because it is taken by everybody concerned as a matter of course; and if some one got up a carnival at Blackpool we should feel, not that it would necessarily be worse done, but that however well it was done it would lack the one thing that makes a carnival attractive. It would be like hiring a man to jodel on the Keswick coach.

This peculiar type of natural beauty is not confined to rural life; it is equally found in the life of towns, so far as these towns are felt to be remote from the bustle and sophistication of our own modern town-life. If a name for it is necessary, one might perhaps, though not without hesitation, make use of the word picturesque; for that word clearly denotes a form of natural beauty, since the essence of the picturesque is the spectator's sense of a gulf between the object and his own habitual surroundings and activities, and at the same time the word is applied indifferently to natural objects and to the life and works of man.

The love of natural beauty is often regarded as a peculiarly modern thing, a fruit of our urban and industrial civilization. If nature means the picturesque, this is true; or rather, it is true that the industrializing of our civilization has produced a new form of the picturesque, and has concentrated our feeling for natural beauty upon the spectacle of a rural society living in the pursuit of traditional arts and deeply rooted in a landscape which has in part created it and in part been created by it. Such a society is the pit whence we were digged; it is what we all were before the industrial revolution; and when that event had divorced us from this state of things, our civilization began to feel its own industrialism as artificial and the pre-industrial society of the countryside and the little town as natural and, therefore, as endowed with all the peculiar qualities of natural beauty. This feeling created for itself a mouthpiece in Wordsworth, and for the last century and a half the movement announced by Wordsworth has steadily increased in depth and strength. To this can be traced all the modern interest in ballad-literature and folk-song and peasant arts, the taste for cottage architecture, the instinctive reversion of town-bred people to country pursuits, and the attempt to preserve beautiful places from being trampled out of existence by the overflow of town life.

This movement is by far the most important fact in the aesthetic life of our own country at the present day; to say nothing of other countries; for the earlier rise of industrialism in England led to an earlier development of this feeling among ourselves. People who think that the aesthetic life means cultivating poetry and endowing opera-houses are apt to believe that the English of to-day are an inartistic race, and even to feel puzzled by the fact that Shakespeare, Purcell, and Turner were Englishmen. But the aesthetic energy of modern England is concentrated upon a very widespread and very profound love of nature, and nature for us means what it meant to Wordsworth, not the opposite of man but the opposite of industrialized man. According to our means and our education, we prefer Hampstead Heath or the Cornish coast or the Lake District or Switzerland ; but the same impulse drives us all. Our first thought, when holiday-time comes round, is to flock into the country ; and we do this not in order to stretch our legs or to repair our health, but in order to enjoy the beauty of the country. If we wanted exercise, we could get it in our towns, like the ancient Greeks ; if we were anxious about our health, we could live more healthily all the year round ; but we will forgo exercise and overwork ourselves for the most part of our time in order to see the country from a cottage-window at week-ends, or travel from Manchester to Bournemouth and back in a motor coach, or take the steamer to Rothesay, or go to the Tirol for a month. Every class of society does these things, and if we were not obsessed by the false philosophy of art which we have inherited from nineteenth-century aestheticism, we should see that in all classes alike the motive of these vast mass-movements is purely aesthetic.

It is the more important that we should understand the basis and the limitations of this motive. It is sometimes supposed that to find a primitive society beautiful implies a sentimental blindness to its defects ; that to discover that the people whom one regards as picturesque are unhappy, underfed, spiteful, lazy, and immoral destroys the sense of their beauty. But this is not so. It is not when the village girl drowns her illegitimate baby that she ceases to be beautiful, but when she dresses in what she takes to be fashionable clothes; it is not when the cottage becomes leaky or verminous that it loses its picturesqueness, but when it is adorned with china cats and fortified with a corrugated iron roof. Nor is it a valid criticism of this attitude to point out— what is quite true—that it objects to the railway and the gasometer because they are innovations, but does not object to the enclosed fields, the two-storied cottages, the metalled country lanes, and the stone churches, which were equally innovations in their time. The lover of the picturesque is no blind *laudator temporis acti*. He does not praise beauty because it is traditional, but tradition because it has created beauty; he loves the cottage and hates the gasometer quite consistently, because the cottage falls into its place in the landscape and the gasometer does not.

But it is true that the love of the picturesque is a self-contra-dictory attitude and one which is bound to destroy what it loves by the very fact that it loves it. The motor-coach that ruins the beauty of the country lane and the hotel that destroys the pic-turesqueness of the Alpine village have been created and launched on their work of destruction by the love of what they have destroyed. It is because Wordsworth has taught so many people to see beauty in the Lake District that the Lake District which he enjoyed no longer exists; the same thing has happened in Switzerland, on the Riviera, and wherever beauty of this peculiar kind has been discovered and enjoyed. The discovery is made by some adventurous spirit who penetrates to a place where the scenery is untouched by the hard lines of road and railway, the architecture unspoilt by the intrusion of hotels and villas, the people unaffected in their manners, primitively hospitable, and picturesquely clad without self-consciousness; and thereupon writes to his friends, with Sophoclean irony, ' this place is perfect; no one ever comes here '. But, unseen by himself, he has gone there; he is already the one blot on that landscape, the one note out of tune in that pastoral symphony ; he is the thin end of the wedge, and his own praises drive the wedge home. He is the spy sent out in advance by the mob of trippers and bank-holiday makers, and he has no choice but either to encourage others to continue the work of destruction which he has begun, or to incur the just reproach of wishing to prevent others from sharing in what he regards as the most precious of pleasures.

This is why those who live in beautiful places for the sake of their beauty are jealous lovers, and hostile towards all who wish to follow them. They fight, and cannot help fighting, against the incursion of railways and motor roads, against the increase of building and the organization of cheap trips ; but they are traitors to their own cause, for they are themselves nothing but squatting trippers, centres of infection where the artificial life which they represent has broken through its barriers into the picture which they wish to enjoy. Their own houses and gardens are already a fatal blot on the landscape ; their own parasitic presence is already a corruption of the traditional life of the people.

This is inevitable, because the beauty of the picturesque is a beauty created by a contrast between the spectator and his object. It is only because we feel ourselves the creatures of a sophisticated civilization that we enjoy the spectacle of a relatively unsophisticated life ; if we lost that feeling, we should lose the pleasure which we now take in the picturesque. Hence we must, in order to sustain that pleasure, sustain in ourselves the feeling of separation from our object ; we must live in the country without becoming countrymen, just as, in order to taste the peculiar pleasure of being on foreign soil, we must live abroad without becoming foreigners ; or as, in order to feel the picturesqueness of a cathedral, we must visit it without being worshippers. To see anything as a thing of natural beauty, we must look upon it with consciously alien eyes ; and therefore, when this object is a human society, we must resist absorption into this society and perpetually assert our alienation from it. This means the maintenance of a discordant note which, because its maintenance is essential to our own sense of the music's beauty, we do not feel as discordant : yet however blind the individual spectator may be to his own destructive influence upon the object which he is enjoying, he cannot be blind to the similar influence of others.

(*c*) But there is a third beauty which must be called a kind of natural beauty : the negation not of all human activity, nor yet of artificiality, but of the conscious intention to be beautiful. If artificiality means the departure from that bondage to natural conditions which characterizes a primitive society, an artificial civilization will necessarily destroy the beauty of primitive society even while it creates the enjoyment of that beauty ; but yet its products have a beauty of their own which is not the beauty of art. The railway and the steamship and the factory are the negation of natural beauty in the senses in which we have hitherto discussed it, but they are beautiful, and their beauty is not, like that of a work of art, an intentional and designed beauty. They are meant to be useful, to carry out certain purposes as efficiently as possible ; yet this very utilitarianism produces beauty at unawares, a beauty which, in its unconsciousness of itself, has the same essential character as that of a mountain or a field of wheat. Hence their beauty is dependent upon the singleness of aim with which their designer has bent himself upon the task of efficiency ; power and speed, economy and strength, perfect adaptation of means to end, generate an austere grace and harmony which can only be disturbed by any conscious effort after decoration. An engineered road destroys the lines of a mountain as completely as a mill destroys the shape of a valley ; yet the road's purposeful line and the mill's blockish building and pointing chimney have a beauty of their own, which may easily be spoilt by giving the

road a rustic parapet and the mill a crenellated outline in a mis-
guided attempt to embellish them. Such embellishment does not
prevent the destruction of beauties to which, in any form, the
road and the mill must be fatal; it merely prevents a new beauty
from coming into existence. So the first motor-cars tried to save
the beauty of the horse-drawn carriage, and only succeeded in being
ridiculous; whereas the motor-car of to-day is only trying to be
itself, and is therefore as beautiful as the *Aquitania* or the Lots
Road power-station.

The subtle affinity between this form of beauty and that which
was last described arises out of the principle that nature is only
conquered by obeying her. The lines of a factory-chimney,
a dam, a fast steamship, are so nicely adjusted to the natural
forces which they are designed to counteract that they present
to the eye visible graphs of these forces; as the curve and stoop
of a sail make the wind visible, so these other lines make visible
the weight of bricks, the thrust of standing water and the resis-
tances of a disturbed liquid. Therefore these utilitarian devices
for overcoming nature are infected with a tang of nature herself,
and in so far as they are beautiful, their beauty is a reflection,
perhaps a concentrated and intensified reflection, of nature's
beauty. And this, again, is the reason why even in this third
form natural beauty is a fragile thing, a thing to be enjoyed in
silence for fear of breaking the charmed sleep on which it depends;
because if the engineer is told that his works are beautiful, and
reacts to the knowledge by aiming henceforth at beauty, employ-
ing architects and artists to collaborate in his designs, he will
infallibly spoil them. He will lapse into the Wardour Street of
engineering, and end as a designer of steam yachts.

4

The Work of Art

§ 17. *The Birth of Art.*—The forms of natural beauty discussed in the last chapter make up a continuous line pointing in a definite direction. In the transition from the first form to the second, and from the second to the third, a principle is gradually emerging which, when it comes into the full light of day, puts an end to the privileged position of nature in the world of the aesthetic consciousness. This principle is that man can create beautiful objects ; or rather, that his creativity is always and essentially a creation of beautiful objects. Human action, which at first appeared as a canker of ugliness distorting and defiling by degrees the face of the world, has been found capable not indeed of ceasing to destroy what is beautiful but of creating fresh beauties ; first the beauty of a primitive society nestling against the bosom of nature, and then the beauty of a sophisticated civilization that has learnt to overcome nature by obeying her. But since the difference between a primitive and an advanced civilization is only one of degree, and every society regards itself as advanced and its predecessors as primitive, the cycle of the three forms is always complete at every point of the historical process ; and therefore the principle of man's power to create beauty is always written large across human experience.

The recognition of this principle is the birth of art, in the narrower and stricter sense of the word. The designer of a power-station or a railway viaduct is an artist, but not a conscious artist : he is creating beauty, but not purposely. He becomes an artist in the strict sense by becoming a conscious artist.

When first we become conscious of our own activities we generally become less efficient in them ; our self-consciousness upsets the instinctive balance and precision of our act, and we appear to have lost a faculty instead of improving it. A person who has never learnt to box or to sing or to practise farming, but has fought and sung and farmed as he picked up the art in every-day experience, is far more efficient than when first he begins to take lessons and tries to box or to sing or to farm scientifically. While he did not think about it, he did it reasonably well; when he starts thinking about it, everything goes wrong. But if we go on thinking, the first disastrous results of thought wear off; we not only form fresh habits, which become as spontaneous as those with which we began, and are developed to a higher pitch, but we also acquire the power to act in circumstances that lie outside our experience, and thus extend indefinitely the range of our faculty as well as intensifying its efficiency in any given field.

The transition from unconscious to conscious art is no exception to this rule. We become aware that we have been producing beautiful objects; for instance, beautiful gestures designed merely—so far as they were designed at all—to convey a meaning to our neighbours, or beautiful houses designed merely to keep out the wind and the rain. We then try to do the same thing consciously; and this first deliberate attempt at art seems to destroy natural beauty without creating anything else. Our gestures become awkward; our houses acquire an air of posturing and leering like the shapeless creatures of a nightmare. There is always something disheartening in such a change, and when we see it on a large scale we are apt to regard it as a sign that a whole civilization has lost its aesthetic faculty. But what appears as the morbid perversion of a taste hitherto pure is in reality nothing but the birth of art. Art, in the narrower sense of the word, the conscious pursuit of beauty, is here seen in the very act of emerging from the chrysalis of nature. This does not mean that the aesthetic consciousness emerges from something other than itself; that, for instance, a purely utilitarian society at a given moment achieves sufficient wealth and leisure to devote some of its time to the enjoyment of beauty; for the aesthetic consciousness is the absolutely primary and fundamental form of all consciousness, and all other forms emerge out of it. Nor does it mean that there is any one historical period at which the aesthetic consciousness passes over from the phase of natural beauty to the phase of artistic beauty : to ask when this happens, or happened, is like asking when a river plunged over a waterfall. It is a transition which is always going on and has always been going on, and is none the less a real transition.

§ 18. *The Work of Art in its Immaturity.*—The birth of art has already taken place when a child covers a piece of paper with meaningless pencil scribbles. These scribbles are not on the same footing as the child's scream of anger or cry of joy, or the movements, often very beautiful, by which it gives vent to its feelings and energies. All these acts are below the line which divides nature from art ; they may be beautiful, but they are not done because they are beautiful. They are the natural foundation of art, beautiful to the spectator with the beauty of nature, but precisely lacking that self-conscious purpose which is absent in nature but present in art. A child scribbles on paper not as an unreflective way of giving vent to its energies but because it finds an aesthetic pleasure in the scribble ; the scribble is intended to be beautiful, and is therefore at a higher level of activity than the jump of joy. It is easy for the adult spectator to overlook this, because the adult spectator sees beauty in the jump of joy and none in the scribble, and therefore, from his own point of view, prefers the former. And certainly the jump of joy is in itself a more finished product than the scribble ; yet it is only nature, whereas the scribble is art ; and nature must reach maturity before she can conceive and bring forth even the feeblest infant art.[1]

[1] A child may scribble not because it finds its scribble beautiful, but because it is pretending to be Daddy writing books or painting pictures. In that case the situation is complicated by an element of imitation, which will be discussed later. The case considered in the text is that of a child which is not consciously imitating any one or anything, but simply enjoying the act of making pencil lines on paper.

The scribble is the work of art in its most rudimentary form; and the same form reappears in acts like swinging a leg or stamping a foot, beating a drum or blowing a tin trumpet, singing or whistling in a random and tuneless fashion, and countless other acts that may be noticed in all children and all adults. These acts are rudimentary works of art in so far as they are conscious sources of aesthetic pleasure; but on so low a level that they are often reprehended as fidgeting or suppressed as nuisances. Even the rhythmic movements of breathing or walking may become aesthetic acts by being tuned to a conscious rhythm, as in marching: a column of men on the march is an orchestra in which every instrument is a primitive drum.

But the work of art at this level is only a rudimentary work of art, because it is a random and uncontrolled production, enjoyed only so long as we do not care whether it is done well or ill. The scribbling child takes pleasure in his scribble just because it is a scribble, not because it is a good scribble; the note required of the tin trumpet is just any note, of any quality, any duration and any intensity; the drum is pleasant because it makes a bang, not because it makes one kind of bang rather than another. This undiscriminating joy in the production of anything whatever, not because it is this thing rather than that thing, but because it is simply, in the abstract, something produced, is the bare minimum of art in the stricter sense: the beautiful is here anything which we ourselves produce, and the aesthetic enjoyment is the bare sense of our own creativeness.

This feeling is not only enhanced, but acquires a new quality, when by repeating such acts we learn to control them and modify them in definite ways. This control is the technical element in art. Technique is based on the realization by rudimentary art of its need for self-discipline, which depends on a growing dissatisfaction with bare creation and a desire to develop the power of creating this thing rather than that thing.

The acquisition of technique is what we call learning to draw, learning to sing, and so forth : and this means learning not how to make marks and noises, but how to make certain marks and certain noises. To be engaged on the task of acquiring technique in a deliberate and conscious manner is to be a student. The child who is not yet a student is unconsciously acquiring technique by merely going on scribbling ; and the skilled artist has never finished perfecting his technique ; but ' study ' in the special sense is an activity whose essence is concentration on the technical element in art, and the philosophy of the art-school is therefore the philosophy of technique.

Technique means, primarily, the muscular control which enables the creator to create exactly what he wants : draw the right line, sing the right note, and so forth. But secondarily, it is a training not of the muscles but of the eye and ear, or, more precisely, of the imagination, by which we become able to discriminate shades of form and sound which previously we had not observed to be distinct. Now this control can only be gained by the performance of set tasks. In order to check our ability to do exactly what we want, we must first know what exactly it is that we want, and we must then be able to compare this with what we have done. Otherwise, whatever line we draw may be, by an easy self-deception, represented as the very line we wanted to draw. Hence technique can only be acquired by copying ready-made models, and these models must be, not natural objects, but works of art. The singing-master must sing a note for his pupil to imitate, and tell him when he does it badly ; the drawing master must show his pupil how to draw by drawing. A student is as likely to learn drawing by being set face to face with nature as he is to learn Greek by being left alone with a plain text of Homer. No doubt a very clever student might, in such circumstances, find out how to draw for himself ; but the teacher's business is to supply grammar and dictionary. Nor must the difference between the aim and nature of a student's drawing and a master's sketch be forgotten. It cannot be too clearly understood that a student's drawing is a technical exercise and not a work of art. It has no business to be beautiful; its business is to be accurate; and if it is called beautiful, this is only because accuracy itself is aesthetically felt as a peculiar kind of beauty. No art master would praise or blame the work of his students on any ground but this, and a student who takes the same liberties with his copy that an artist takes with his subject is trying to run before he can walk.

But the imitativeness of students' work is of value in developing and strengthening the creative faculty precisely because it is not pure imitation but disguised creation. You can make a novice climb by roping him and leading him; he supports himself because he thinks some one else is supporting him. This applies to all education. The student is really painting pictures of his own; his own hand and eye are doing the work, and the copy is only setting the pace. When the student awakes to the consciousness of this truth, he is no longer a student, but has graduated as a master.

§ 19. *Formal Art.*—The child's scribble, after passing through the fire of technical training, emerges as a formal work of art, a skilfully-drawn scribble, that is, a pattern. So with the arts of song and gesture. The formal art of patterns, in whatever material, is the simplest type of mature and skilled art; for a pattern is a work of art in its greatest possible degree of simplicity, a work of art which owes nothing to any experience except itself.

But form is correlative to matter, and all artistic production, so far as it is formal, is the control and disposal of this or that material. There must be some material, for this material is at bottom nothing else than the nature which, as we have seen, is the presupposition of art: not the presupposition of the aesthetic activity in general, for that has no presuppositions, but the presupposition of the specific form of that activity which is art in the strict sense. Formal art, then, is the imposition of a specified form on a given matter, but this act is not the first appearance of beauty, for the matter is itself nothing but natural beauty, and that is why it can be raised to a higher power by the skill of the artist.

It is the essence of matter that it should consist of an endless plurality of distinctions. The patterns of formal art therefore embody themselves in materials whose variousness is of their very essence as materials ; and this is the source of the plurality of the ' arts ', painting, music, poetry, sculpture, dancing, gardening, and so on *ad infinitum*. There must be an indefinite number of these, and it cannot be possible to arrange them in a logical scheme, precisely because they represent the indefinite plurality of matter as opposed to the organized unity of form.

But the material is not purely passive to the activity of the artist. Just because it has already its own natural beauty, it insists upon being handled in one way rather than another ; and this recalcitrance, which is a handicap to a bad artist, becomes a positive source of inspiration to a good one. The artist studies his material and learns the ' feel ' of it : he defers to it and asks it for advice as to how best he may handle it. Nor is he left alone with his material ; his work is always influenced by the traditions of design in which he has been brought up. Nothing in the whole history of art is more striking than the way in which, out of the infinite number of possible patterns, the artists of a certain period confine themselves to a tiny common stock which they modify very slowly and by very small changes. Thus tradition becomes a standard, and a special form like the fugue imposes itself upon a school in such a way that music comes to mean the fugue and musical beauty comes to mean conformity with the fugal standard. Hence we ask ourselves, concerning a given piece of design, not simply whether it is beautiful, but whether it observes the rules of its special form. Such a question is right and necessary, though it may easily become pedantic unless the critic realizes that the rules are not an external limit to the artist's work, but a presupposition which that work absorbs into itself; that in the actual life of an artistic tradition the rules are neither pedantically obeyed nor anarchically flouted, but reinterpreted and created afresh by each new member of the school in whose life the tradition lives.

The artist who has mastered the feel of his material and the style of his school produces works which are no longer mere patterns, nor yet patterns crippled by the forces of material and tradition, but patterns deliberately based on and expressing these forces. A work of this kind cannot be understood or appreciated except by reference to the medium and the stylistic tradition. A marble statue, a violin sonata, or a Greek tragedy is the fruit of specialized training, and its beauty cannot be felt except by going through a specialized training. This does not imply that the artist or the spectator, in the actual moment of creation or enjoyment, is thinking about materials and rules. His experience of these things, as exemplified in other works of art, presents itself in this moment as a feeling colouring his aesthetic activity. The work of art remains a monad : the artist in creating it is aware of it only, and is not thinking of precedents, conventions, or earlier essays in the same material. But these things have actually conditioned his work ; they are the stepping-stones by which he has reached this point of view ; and they survive in the work of art, transmuted into the form of aesthetic experience. And it is precisely by having reflected on these things that the artist strengthens and develops this aesthetic experience. By knowing his own relation to his materials and tradition, by being the historian or critic of his own art, he becomes a competent artist, the master instead of the slave of his materials and tradition. Here, as at a previous stage (§ 14), reflection upon imagination colours imagination itself.

§ 20. *Naturalistic Art.*—Naturalistic art is not an attempt to reproduce nature but an attempt to depict it. A painter does not try to reproduce a mountain or a table, which would mean making another mountain or another table : an actor does not try to reproduce a murder, which would mean committing another murder. A mountain can be represented by a painter, and a murder by an actor, without any multiplication of geographical features or deaths. To depict an object is to produce, not another of its kind, but a work of art resembling it ; depiction is the creation, in a different material, of a formal pattern suggested by the original object. Formal art is the creation of patterns suggested by the possibilities of the material and by other patterns in the same tradition : naturalistic art adds another source of suggestion, namely a natural object. Naturalistic art is thus formal art fertilized by natural beauty.

It might be thought that this additional source added nothing new to the aesthetic character of the work of art, because a suggestion is still a suggestion, whether it arises from art or from nature. But this would be a mistake. To create a work of art on the strength of a suggestion given by another work *in pari materia* is not only much easier than to do so on the strength of a suggestion given by a natural object—which is why the work of young artists is generally imitative, based on a knowledge of art rather than on a knowledge of nature—but it is easier because it differs in kind, it is a more elementary type of activity. Naturalism is a more advanced phase of artistic work than formalism. A ' conventionalized ' drawing of a natural object—the human figure, for example, reduced to geometrical terms—is not necessarily a degraded version of a ' naturalistic ' drawing. In general, the reverse is the case. A child begins drawing people in a purely ' conventionalized ' manner, and its drawings only become naturalistic as it learns to draw better. The transition from conventionalized to naturalistic representation of objects is an artistic advance; the transition from naturalistic to conventional, an artistic decline.

Naturalistic art is a modification of formal art; but this modification does not take place at a high level of development only. As there is a rudimentary type of formal art which is found at a very low level, so there is a rudimentary naturalism which is found wherever sufficient control has been acquired to permit its occurrence. As soon as a child has learnt to make one noise rather than another at will, it copies noises; for instance, a child eight months old, if it has a good ear, will imitate a motor-horn; and the proverbial imitativeness of children is due not to an 'instinct' of imitation—such instincts are the *asylum ignorantiae* of bankrupt psychologies—but to the emergence of the naturalistic element in their imaginative life. Just as there is a constant overflow of aesthetic activity into outward expression, as we never enjoy any aesthetic experience without some play of gesture, a movement of the limbs, a smile or a frown, or the like, so there is a constant tendency for this outward expression to imitate the object in a material of our own: we gesticulate at a landscape, stamp our feet to music, and so forth.

Naturalistic art is an attempt to copy nature; but this is to attempt the impossible. Nature is so infinitely rich in detail, so infinitely subtle in her effects, that we cannot really copy her. The naturalistic artist is like a man writing a piano version of an orchestral score; he has to leave out practically everything, and misrepresent everything he puts in. And the harder we try to copy nature, the farther we get from her true spirit; because the meticulous elaboration of detail produces an effect of labour which is the precise opposite of the effortless fertility of natural detail. But if we cannot copy nature in her entirety, we must select; and selecting is idealizing, for the omission of some part of the object is not mere omission of a part but alteration of the whole. Naturalistic art is thus forced to idealize, consciously or unconsciously ; and the only question is on what principle this idealizing is to be done. If nature is to be the artist's guide—an assumption essential to naturalistic art—nature must herself supply the principle. We must alter nature by reference to nature, which can only mean altering this particular instance of nature by reference to others. But what others ? Every particular instance of nature is equally impossible to copy and therefore equally in need of idealization ; and it follows that the criterion of idealization must be found in a purely ideal nature. What we are to depict, then, is a typical or generalized nature which is nowhere actual ; and we alter the particular objects which we are ostensibly copying so as to bring them nearer to conformity with this norm or type. That artists actually do this will be questioned by no one who has any acquaintance with, for instance, the history of portrait-painting.

But the norm or ideal by reference to which we idealize nature is not actually found in nature at all. We may imagine it to be reached by an inductive study of individual objects, but this is simply an error. Nothing could be more palpably false than that a portrait-painter leaves out from the portrait of a lady every detail in which she differs from the other ladies he has seen. The ideal in question is an ideal of the imagination, created by itself for its own guidance ; a law laid down wholly *a priori*, and independently of all experience of the natural world, by the pure act of the aesthetic spirit.

§ 21. *Imaginative Art.*—At this point the naturalistic idea of art overthrows itself, and the discovery is made that naturalism rests on a principle of which it can give no account, namely the idealization of nature by a pure *a priori* act of imagination. The recognition of this truth brings us to the culminating phase of artistic creation, which for lack of a better name we may call imaginative art : the art in which the autonomy and self-sufficiency of imagination are vindicated and the naturalistic element is reabsorbed. A marble Aphrodite is at once a pattern in marble, because it stands or falls by the balance of its masses and the harmony of its lines, and a copy, because it reproduces the pattern which the artist found in a female figure. It idealizes that pattern, as any copy must ; and so far, it does not differ from a naturalistic work of art. Where it differs is that it idealizes consciously. In carving a portrait-head the artist is idealizing, for he cannot help it, but he thinks he is copying ; in carving an Aphrodite he knows that he is idealizing. By this knowledge he sets himself free from that servitude to idealization which we call mannerism. The portrait-painter has mannerisms which make him unconsciously alter the shape of an eye-socket, the profile of a nose, the position of a mouth ; and these to some extent impair the perfection of every naturalistic work of art, regarded as naturalistic. But in the imaginative work of art they are no longer a handicap but an inspiration. As an artist masters his material by finding out what it can do, instead of trying to make it do what it cannot, so he masters his mannerisms not by eradicating them—for he would always develop others—but by converting them into merits, inventing imaginary figures in which these mannerisms, given free play, become beauties.

To say that the artist knows that he is idealizing does not mean that the actual work of aesthetic creation includes knowledge as part of itself. That is impossible ; the work of art is always an act of imagination, not of thought. What is meant is that the act includes a feeling which, when analysed, reveals itself as an intuitive awareness of idealization : whereas the naturalistic artist does not experience this feeling, though analysis shows that he too is actually idealizing. Now when we feel a thing intuitively, this may mean that we have already explicitly known it, and it has come to colour our feelings ; or that it is a mere feeling which has never reached the level of thought but is, as we sometimes say, ' instinctive '. Is it because the artist, as critic or historian of his own work, has become reflectively aware that he has been idealizing, or is it merely ' instinctively ', that the feeling arises in him which prompts him to desert naturalistic for imaginative art ?

This question can be answered by considering the function of the title attached to a work of art. The title of a portrait implies that the artist not only is trying to copy something, but has reflected on his work and has explicitly discovered that he is trying to do so. The title of an imaginative work, for instance of a statue called Aphrodite, implies that the artist knows himself to have arrived at this aesthetic experience not by copying but by reimagining the beauty of the female figure and of a certain group of artistic works. Had he not reflectively known this, he might have carved the statue, but he would not have given it the name. The name implies a reference beyond the single aesthetic act ; but the act itself has no such reference ; the reference is therefore the work of reflective thought. The title of a work of art is an historical note explaining how the artist arrived at this point of view, and intended to help others to reach the same point. In so far as the statue is felt to need a title, the achievement of this monadic point of view is conditioned not merely by having passed through certain other experiences but by the artist's knowledge that he has done so.

The ' subject ' of a work of art is a similar reference from the work itself to the series of aesthetic experiences through which it was achieved. When people ask what a work of art ' is about ', they are trying to get an orientation or point of view from which to contemplate it. From its own point of view, the imaginative work of art is not ' about ' anything ; it is only a naturalistic work of art that deliberately refers to a subject ; but from the reflective point of view every work of art may be said to have a subject in so far as it is a resultant of certain experiences other than itself.

It may be asked at this point how imaginative art differs from formal art; for if the naturalistic element is reabsorbed, if the beauty of a statue depends wholly on the balance of its masses and the harmony of its lines, as was said at the beginning of this section, it might appear that the statue is after all a pure pattern and nothing but a pattern, in which case what has here been called imaginative art is nothing but formal art over again. In a sense this is true; the imaginative work of art does not appeal, in order to explain its own beauty or to excuse its own ugliness, to the naturalistic principle that the object depicted ' was so ', but feels itself perfectly free to depart from the object wherever this fails to satisfy its own imaginative standard of beauty. But none the less there is a perfectly definite distinction between formal and imaginative art, which may be seen by reflecting on their presuppositions. Formal art in its perfection presupposes that, first, the artist's materials, and secondly, the traditional rules of the form in which he works, have been so far mastered by his own efforts that they have become, as Beethoven said of the rules of music, his very obedient humble servants. Imaginative art presupposes this and also a further training, namely a training in naturalistic art. Naturalistic art in its whole extent is, from the point of view of imaginative art, a training, a process of discipline and education by which the artist absorbs the entire range of natural beauty into the materials of his work. And since, as has already been pointed out, the transition from formal to naturalistic art is a necessary transition, necessitated by the fundamental character of imagination itself, the return from naturalism to a new formalism in the shape of imaginative art is not only necessary in its turn, but gives rise to a new kind of art, which is not impelled to pass over into naturalistic art but has conquered that impulse by having gone through it and out to the other side, and is therefore its own master.

5

The Life of Art

§ 22. *The Work of Art and the Life of Art.*—The creation of works of art is not the ultimate aim or crowning phase of the aesthetic life. It is a necessary phase of that life, and a phase which is never transcended, but one whose position in the life of art as a whole is quite secondary, and whose necessity is the necessity of a means rather than that of an end.

The question why a painter paints is not an unanswerable question, as it would be if painting were the real aim and end of the painter's activity. He paints in order to see. Until one has drawn it, one does not know what a thing is like ; one has not observed it with that combination of attention to detail and attention to general effect which alone deserves the name of seeing. A person who does not draw has only a dim and vague feeling of the look of things, and at no single point has he a clear or accurate grasp of their appearance. At was observed in § 18, learning to draw means at bottom learning to see ; and the whole of painting consists in an attempt on the part of the painter to force upon himself a habit of precise observation. This progressive sharpening of vision is an infinite process ; for as soon as the possibilities of precision in one direction seem likely to be exhausted, a different line of development suggests itself. Thus a painter who has done his utmost in observing detail may awake to the possibility of seeing relations between broad masses ; in attending to colours he may have failed to notice the varying textures of things, and so forth. Similarly, the practice of music is a sharpening of our discrimination with regard to the pitch, intensity, quality and inter-relations of sounds ; the drama and the novel perform the same function with regard to human nature. And in all these and like cases, the artist himself is intuitively aware of the instrumental character of his works. An artist does not want to build himself a picture-gallery in which to hang his own paintings, in order to enjoy their beauty. He prefers to stow them away in a lumber-room, or let other people look at them. To be compelled to look at them himself would be torment. The act of creation once over, the real product of this act is the continued and intensified activity, which has reached a new phase of its development by merely having passed through the old : and the artist now wants to begin painting another picture. The picture which he is about to paint is always going to be his masterpiece ; that which he has lately finished is always a disheartening daub ; those which he painted years ago are monuments of a distant youth upon which he looks back with mixed feelings, toleration and complacency, a little admiration and a little contempt.

The work of art is thus a phase in a dialectical process in which the aesthetic spirit by its own labour continually grows upon itself. As the ultimate standard by which the work of art is shaped is the pure act of imagination, so the life to whose advancement the work is an instrument is the pure life of imagination ; for when an artist says that he paints in order to enable himself to see, this seeing is not the perceptual seeing of the common-sense consciousness, but simply imagination.

But the life of imagination is a life in which all human beings participate. Hence the work which the artist creates in order to advance his own aesthetic life is in principle capable of the same function in any one else's aesthetic life. In the act itself, this truth is not explicitly present. The artist does not paint for an audience, but for himself ; and it is only by truly satisfying himself that he can truly satisfy others. But what he is trying to satisfy in himself is, whether he knows it or not, that imaginative activity which is the same in himself as in others ; and it is no more possible that a work of art should be truly and ultimately beautiful to one person and not to others than that a scientific demonstration should be truly and ultimately cogent to one

person and not to others. In both cases alike there are vast
divergences between different people's requirements and satis-
factions; but the principle at work in these divergences is the
same in the two cases, and there is no more real difference of
opinion as to the merits of Sophocles than of Aristotle, of
Shakespeare than of Newton.

It is the implicit conviction of this truth that impels the artist
to publish or exhibit his works, and to attach some importance to
their reception. In making the work he has been trying to see
something for himself; in publishing, he is trying to show the
same thing to others.

§ 23. *Genius and Taste: The Classics.*—The person to whom
a work of art is exhibited, if it actually succeeds in conveying its
point of view to him, has achieved a step forward in the dialectic
of his own aesthetic life by its help. He therefore regards it as
his master, as something from which he has learnt what he could
not find out for himself. Between him and it there is the dialectical relation of patient to agent, a person who can follow
and a person who can lead. This relation appears in every type
of activity, art and science, religion and morals, economics and
politics; and in art it takes the special form of the relation
between taste and genius. Genius is the active or creative faculty,
taste the passive or receptive; but they are not two faculties but
two correlative phases of the single aesthetic activity, for the
essence of genius is that it can lead taste, the essence of taste is
that it can follow genius. Yet there is a real gulf between them,
the eternal gulf between master and pupil, prophet and disciple,
ruler and subject. The distinction is not one of degree; for
though it is based upon a greater intensity of aesthetic activity
on the one hand and a less on the other, it consists essentially not
in this inequality itself, but in the recognition of the inequality
and a deliberate adjustment of the inferior to his position.

The attitude of discipleship to certain artists erects these into

the position of ' classics ' or ' masters ' in the technical aesthetic sense. No one is a classic or a master in himself, but only in virtue of the habitual belief that we who call him so are permanently inferior to him in aesthetic power, and can take up towards him no attitude but that of learner or follower. To speak of the classics is to acquiesce in the conviction that one cannot create great works of art for oneself, though one has the taste to recognize them when one sees them ; to claim for oneself at most the position of a minor artist whose achievements must always be immeasurably surpassed by those of one's masters.

This reverence for the work of others is a necessary phase in any healthy and progressive artistic life ; a man must be a very bad artist indeed if he never, at any time of his life, thinks that Homer and Titian and Bach have done better work than anything he is likely to do. Yet there is a certain confusion in this attitude of unquestioning reverence towards the classics, and therefore a certain instability.

§ 24. *The Revolt against the Classics.*—If taste were irrevocably inferior to genius, it could not even pay that respect to genius by which alone it is recognized as taste. A great man is great by thinking great thoughts ; and if we cannot think his thoughts, we cannot know his greatness. But if we can think them, we raise ourselves to his level and become great also. This reflection cannot be dismissed by the argument that we think these thoughts only when we blindly accept what he tells us, and not by any power proper to ourselves ; for if that were so, we should swallow everything that anybody told us with the same blind gratitude, and thus taste would be merely lack of discrimination, or lack of taste. To distinguish great from small we may indeed remain inferior to the great, but we must rise above the small ; and then the only question is where to draw the line. Wherever we draw it, it must be a line to whose altitude we have flown on our own wings.

In short, only genius can understand genius. An inferior mind drags down the objects of its admiration to its own level. That aesthetic consciousness which labels itself as taste is really genius ignorant of its own nature; it thinks of itself as merely receptive and passive whereas it is in fact creative and active, creative of that standard by which it recognizes certain works as works of genius. In that recognition, the student of the classics thinks that their energy is, as if by magnetic induction, evoking a reflex of it in himself; but it is really his own creative imagination that discovers in their work a mirrored likeness of itself, for he finds in them just what he has in himself.

The advance in his aesthetic life which he had ascribed to the influence of the classics is therefore due simply to his own efforts to understand the classics; and when he discovers this he becomes conscious of his own freedom and power, and ceases to regard the classics as the source of his own activity. This discovery is the germ of that revolt against the classics which is a necessary and perpetually recurring phase of the life of art.[1] The genius, once sublime, becomes ridiculous, and the aesthetic spirit embarks on a campaign of iconoclasm against its own superstitions. It cannot simply ignore the masters whom it has worshipped, because its admiration for them has by its own act become ingrained and inveterate, and it is now bent on liberating itself from this servile attitude. It is fighting against itself, and fighting for its freedom; and the more in earnest it is, the more bitterly it must reject the authority which once it lovingly accepted. The fierceness of this revolt is due to nothing but the strength of the hold which the once accepted master still retains on the loyalty of the rebel. The firmer is this hold, the more violent must be its removal; and hence the revolt against the classics is most intense and most painful precisely in those people who

[1] It might be possible to claim for this permanent aesthetic category the name of Romanticism; but that word in actual usage seems to denote a certain historical period or event.

have best learnt what these classics can teach them, and have most keenly enjoyed the learning of it.

Some such revolt against authority, simply because it is authority, is a universal feature of all spiritual life. It is the counterpart and recoil of the opposite tendency to accept authority simply because it is authority : to obey simply because commands are given. In this blind obedience the spirit is free, for it obeys freely, but it is unaware of its own freedom ; in the recoil from blind obedience to blind revolt it has become not only aware of it but obsessed by it and feverishly impatient of the lightest touch that reminds it of its former subjection. This movement from blind obedience to blind revolt underlies much of what recent psychology has fancifully called the Oedipus complex ; and it is well symbolized by the story of the man who, when charged with beating his father, pleaded in defence that it ran in the family.

But in the mood of revolt the rebel does not realize that he is fighting against his own fixed habits. He thinks he is fighting against a definite and tangible enemy, Victorianism, the Eighteenth Century, Medieval Art, or whatever it may be. He falls into the optical illusion of thinking that all art has its merits except the art of the period immediately preceding his own, and the result of this illusion is always the same, namely that the rebellion against tradition or academicism rushes into the assertion of a new and equally tyrannous tradition, a new and equally narrow academicism. The rebel thus becomes in his turn a tyrant and an object of just hatred to other rebels. This cannot be otherwise, for rebellion is the destruction of what exists merely because it exists, and as soon as it has established itself it has become an existing principle, a system or dogma, and its own spirit is therefore logically committed to its destruction. Rebellion is in fact the purely negative side of all activity. An activity which does not lapse into stagnation must negate that which it is, in order to become that which as yet it is not ; but negation by itself is simply nothing at all; it is annihilation, and therefore the rebel who was a mere rebel would be merely a suicide.

§ 25. *The Life of Art in its Freedom.*—Rebellion is self-destructive, and burns itself out when it has destroyed that against which it is in revolt. The rebel is in revolt against himself, against his own spirit of servility ; and therefore the spirit of servility and the spirit of rebellion expire together. Out of their death a new spirit is born, namely the spirit of freedom. The slave is free, but does not know it ; the rebel is so much obsessed by the idea that he is free, that he cannot enjoy his freedom ; but when we have ceased either blindly to follow our leaders or blindly to fight them, we can at last begin to walk beside them in a new-found friendship.

From this new point of view we can once more enjoy and admire great works of art ; but this is a critical instead of an uncritical admiration. Not that we admire them the less for being critical of them ; on the contrary, we admire them more, because great works become greater to an eye that looks at them through the clear air of candid appraisement instead of the smoke of idolatry.

This attitude may perhaps be described as the attitude of appreciation, the word being used in its proper sense and not as a mere synonym for admiration. To appreciate a work of art is to recognize its aesthetic qualities, to be sensible of its beauty. Every work of art has its beauty, and the attitude of appreciation is the attitude which approaches every work of art with the expectation of finding in it some beauty peculiar to itself. To achieve this attitude is to overcome all those prejudices which lead us to expect certain classes of work to be beautiful and certain other classes ugly ; to approach certain things with a predisposition to find them beautiful because they are Greek, or medieval, or of the Ming dynasty, and other things with a predisposition to find them ugly because they are baroque or Victorian. Every period and school of art is aiming at something, at some peculiar type of effect which it feels to be worth achieving; and to be hostile to any given period or school means to deprive oneself of the aesthetic experience in which that period or school specialized, and so to impoverish one's aesthetic life to just that extent. To achieve this breadth of appreciation is not to be an historian or a critic; it is an aesthetic, not a reflective, activity. But it is the necessary basis for any sound historical or critical work.

The free life of art is this appreciative life, which is acquired by absorbing all that technical training can give, and through this training becoming increasingly sensitive to all beauty in nature and art. Such a life will necessarily produce works of art in its endless round of self-education, but these will be felt as mere points of emphasis or concentration in a process which goes on within the spirit itself; it will necessarily lose itself in admiration of nature and art, but only to recover its balance by finding in its own imagination an enhanced creativity. Its life will be nothing but the ceaseless flow of this creative energy, issuing eternally from its fountain-head in the pure act of imagination, and passing eternally through its cyclical phases, to end eternally as the pure act of imagination again.

To say this is not to describe an abstract or unattainable ideal, a metaphysical figment or a transcendent goal towards which the aesthetic spirit of man is struggling. It is to describe the actual facts which characterize the life of every artist. The life of art in its perfect freedom is that concrete life which every one, so far as he is an artist, enjoys. The unattainable, the illusory, is not this perfect freedom but those mutilated fragments of reality which a superficial analysis mistakes for reality itself: the sublime, the comic, formal art, naturalistic art, classical art, romantic art, and so forth. Yet every one of these is a real and distinguishable element in that pure act which is the free life of art.

6

Art and the Life of the Spirit

§ 26. *The Life of the Spirit : Art and Religion.*—The life of the
spirit is an indivisible whole within which are necessary and permanent distinctions : permanent in the sense that the spirit in
its own activity perpetually reaffirms them, and necessary in the
sense that the attempt not to affirm them would merely result
in affirming them over again. Fundamentally, the spirit is
awareness or consciousness, which implies a *prima facie* distinction
between the conscious spirit and the world of which it is conscious ;
but since this awareness is itself an act, a self-modification on the
part of the spirit, the passivity of pure awareness rests upon the
creativity of action, and the life of the spirit is a whole within
which consciousness and action, awareness of the world and
modification of the world, are correlative elements. The unity
of these two elements is feeling, where that of which we are aware
is our own states, and these states are identical with the feeling
of them : they are at once states of consciousness and objects of
consciousness. Hence a rhythm in which awareness and activity
concentrate themselves into the unity of feeling, and feeling again
articulates itself into awareness and activity, is fundamental in all
aspects of the spiritual life.

But life is not a mere rotation of three psychological categories
in a rhythmical monotony. This triple rhythm is present in all
life, but it is never twice alike ; its whole character is altered by
the specific differences of the experience in which it is embodied.
These differences emerge in the course of a process which on its
theoretical side may be called the spirit's attempt to know itself,
on its practical side the spirit's attempt to create itself. To know
itself means also knowing its world, and to create itself means
creating its world ; its world in the former case means the world
of which it is aware, in the latter case the world in which it can
live. There is a theoretical rhythm in the spirit's life, which

consists of an alternate concentration on the external world and on its own nature, and a practical rhythm, which consists of an alternate adaptation of itself to the world and of the world to its own needs ; and the unity of these two rhythms is an emotional rhythm consisting in the feeling of its unity with the world and its opposition to the world.

The first stage in this process is the life of art, which is the pure act of imagination. This is not only empirically the first stage observable in children and primitive peoples, it is necessarily the first stage. Awareness in itself, in its absolutely undifferentiated immediacy, can only be awareness of that which we immediately apprehend, and unawareness of that which we do not : that is, it is an act of consciousness which presents to itself an object of whose relation to other objects it takes no cognizance. As consciousness ranges over a field of objects, it illuminates that object upon which it falls and leaves all others in total darkness : the immediate object is its whole world and it knows nothing beyond. But this is that monadic consciousness which, as we have seen, is imagination ; and all that has been done in the preceding chapters is to elaborate this concept of imagination and bring out enough of its implications to show its identity with what we ordinarily call the aesthetic experience. Action in itself, the undifferentiated immediacy of the practical life, consists in doing that which we do and nothing else ; that is to say, immersing ourselves in an activity without any question as to the relation between this activity and anything else which at the moment we are not doing. To say this is to describe that form of action which we call play ; and therefore play is the practical aspect of art, art the theoretical aspect of play. What characterizes each is its immediacy, that is to say, its concentration upon the activity of the moment and its ignoring of anything outside this activity. A game is what it is for no reason outside itself ; it is played as if there were nothing in the world but games, and no games but this game.

Just as art does not explain itself by stating reasons, so play does not explain itself by stating reasons ; and immediacy means the absence of reasons.

But this immediacy is not and cannot be a self-contained and complete form of consciousness. To imagine in a concentrated and truly imaginative way, one must know that one is imagining ; and hence imagination rests upon its own opposite, thought. It is only within a consciousness which distinguishes truth from falsehood that we can find in actual existence that consciousness which does not distinguish them. Otherwise a cry of pain or joy would be the whole of poetry, a dream the whole of painting, an instinctive pursuit or flight the whole of dancing. The work of art is related to these things as the vertebrate to the amoeba ; and the skeleton, unseen but indispensable, is thought.

The question ' what am I ? ' can therefore no longer be answered in terms of imagination ; I am not merely an imaginer but a thinker. The question ' what is my world ? ' must be answered by saying that it is a world not merely of fancies but of realities. But if I who think am also the I who imagine, it would seem natural to superimpose the act of thinking on the act of imagining in such a way that the real is merely one division of the imaginary. The only world whose existence we have learned to recognize is the world of our own imaginations ; and when the distinction between reality and unreality forces itself upon us, as it does the instant we come to reflect upon imagination, we impose this distinction upon the world of imaginations, and regard certain imaginations as true and others as false. To do this is to break with the life of art ; for art knows nothing of the distinction, and merely imagines what it imagines and does not imagine what it does not imagine. But now we are asserting one imaginary object as real, and denying another as unreal ; and to do this is to embark upon the life of religion.

It is a commonplace that all religion expresses itself in mythological or metaphorical terms ; it says one thing and means another ; it uses imagery to convey truth. But the crucial fact about religion is not that it is metaphor, but that it is unconscious metaphor. No one can express any thought without using metaphors, but this does not reduce all philosophy and science to religion, because the scientist knows that his metaphors are merely metaphors and that the truth is something other than the imagery by which it is expressed, whereas in religion the truth and the imagery are identified. To repeat the Creed as a religious act it is necessary not to add ' All this I believe in a symbolical or figurative sense ' : to make that addition is to convert religion into philosophy.

Thus in religion that indifference to the distinction between real and unreal, which is the essence of art, is abolished. Religion is essentially a quest after truth and explicitly conscious of itself as such a quest. But the truth which it can and does discover is a truth which is always hidden from view in a reliquary of symbolism : we see the imagery, but we do not see the truth ; we are only conscious that the truth is there, and its presence converts the beauty of the imagery into holiness. But inasmuch as this holiness is a property of a mere symbol, religion always contains an element of idolatry and superstition.

§ 27. *Science, History, Philosophy.*—Religion consists of a perpetual attempt to overcome its own initial error, to destroy superstition and idolatry, to reach the spirit behind the letter. But success in this attempt is the death of religion ; when the metaphor becomes conscious metaphor, when the thought is distinguished from the imagery in which it has been wrapped up, the symbol loses its holiness and becomes merely significant. Language and thought now fall apart, and language becomes the mere instrument of thought. In art the presence of thought— for we saw that thought was present—was wholly forgotten, and the object of attention was pure language, or rather an imagery

which, because not explicitly correlative to thought, was not yet
explicitly language ; in religion thought was immediately identified with the language expressing it, and was therefore never
truly expressed. But with the achievement of that distinction
between letter and spirit which is the goal of religion, we have
reached the life of explicit or self-conscious thought.

To separate thought from language, intellect from imagination,
and to concentrate on thought as distinct from imagination, is
. the characteristic of that type of consciousness which we call
scientific. Here thought is regarded as an activity self-contained
and self-sufficient, and its object as a self-contained and self-
sufficient intelligible world, reached through, but lying behind,
the sensible world. The aim of science is to apprehend this
purely intelligible world as a thing in itself, an object which is
what it is independently of all thinking, and thus antithetical to
the sensible world, which is admittedly relative to our apprehension of it, being in fact nothing else than the world of imagination
which is at once the object and the creature of the imaginative
activity. The world of thought is the universal, the timeless and
spaceless, the absolutely necessary, whereas the world of sense
is the contingent, the changing and moving appearance which
somehow indicates or symbolizes it.

But this very separation of reality from appearance, the necessary from the contingent, creates a problem which to the scientific
consciousness is insoluble. The appearance must somehow be an
appearance of the reality ; the contingent must somehow be
grounded in the necessary. Appearance and reality, imagination
and thought, have been merely distinguished and not related :
they must somehow be brought together again and shown to be
equally necessary, each to the other. This need is satisfied by
the historical consciousness, whose object is the individual ;
no longer an abstract universal divorced from its own equally
abstract particulars, but a universal that particularizes itself,

a particular constituted by its own universality. For history, the truth is no longer an abstract necessity which nowhere actually exists ; it is concrete and actual, it is real in every sense of the word, while the truth of science is a reality which is in one sense utterly unreal, an ideal never realized, a law which has no instances.

Even in history, however, there is a relic of the abstractness of science. This relic consists in the separation of subject and object. The fact which is the object of historical thought is a thing in itself, a thing whose existence and nature are supposed to be wholly independent of the thinker ; the task of the thinker is to discover a world of fact which is ' already there ' for him to discover. And hence there is still in history a failure to realize the unity of thought and action. The historian is a mere spectator, he does not modify the world but apprehends it. He is a man of thought, a student, not a man of action ; and however strongly he feels his kinship with the men of action whose actions he studies, he only feels it and does not actualize it.

This abstractness is only overcome in philosophy. The object of philosophy is nothing short of reality, a reality which includes both the fact of which the historian is aware and his awareness of that fact. The philosopher is the thinker who not only thinks but knows that he thinks and makes it his business to discover the implications of this. He is not, like the historian, outside his own picture ; he sees himself as part of the historical process which he studies, and therefore part of his problem is to understand how that historical process has thrown up in its development an organ—namely himself—which is at once a part of it and the spectator of it. With this clue in his hand, rooted in the fact that he is both the child and the spectator of the historical process, he is able to reinterpret that process itself, and to see in every phase of it a nisus towards self-consciousness. And in realizing that history is the emergence of the spirit's consciousness of itself he is actually achieving that consciousness, and bringing into existence, in his own person, that awareness of itself which he finds to be the fundamental characteristic of spirit. His knowledge is therefore explicitly action; he is creating himself by knowing himself, and so creating for himself an intelligible world, the world of spirit in general.

§ 28. *The Unity of the Spiritual Life.*—The five phases of spiritual life which we have enumerated in this crude outline—and other phases which further analysis might distinguish—are not species of any common genus. They are activities each of which presupposes and includes within itself those that logically precede it; thus religion is inclusively art, science inclusively religion and therefore art, and so on. And on the other hand each is in a sense all that follow it; for instance, in possessing religion we already possess philosophy of a sort, but we possess it only in the form in which it is present in, and indeed constitutes, religion. The unity of the spiritual life is a unity of the same kind as the unity which we have already seen exemplified in the life of art. Art as a whole, we saw, is the pure act of imagination, and this act has its life in a process of self-differentiation and self-concentration, diastole and systole, which generates the various forms and phases of aesthetic activity within the unity of imagination itself, and having generated them treats them as so much material by the mastery of which it vindicates this unity. The act does not find a material, given from without, to unify which is the problem of its life; it generates the material out of itself and thus sets itself the problems which it lives by solving. In the same way the life of the spirit differentiates itself into art, religion, and the rest in order that it may exhibit its own unity in this diversity; or rather, that it may through this diversity bring into existence a unity which is not the bare unity with which it began but a unity enriched by all the differentiations through which it has passed. This process takes place in time, but it is an eternal process : it is always beginning, it has always reached any given point, and it has always arrived at its conclusion, somewhat as—to revert to a previous simile—a river is always rising at its source, always flowing over each part of its course, and always discharging itself into the sea. But because the process of the spirit is a conscious process, like a river which should be aware of itself throughout its course, it does not merely travel through a fixed cycle of changes, but finds every passage past a given point altered in significance by the consciousness of what has gone before it; and hence the unity of the spiritual life resembles the unity of an infinitely increasing spiral rather than the unity of a rotating circle. The energy which causes the spiral to expand is simply that pure activity which is the spirit.

§ 29. *The Mortality and Immortality of Art.*—The spirit is pure act; the aesthetic spirit is the pure act of imagination. But to speak of the pure act of imagination is a contradiction in terms, for the qualification implies a distinction between imagination and thought, and an activity from which another activity is distinguished is by definition not a pure activity but one limited by, because correlative to, another. There is therefore no such thing as this life of pure imagination which is the life of art. Art is not a life but a subordinate element or phase in a life which is indissolubly one, the unitary life of the spirit.

Hence art always has its centre of gravity outside itself. It is not a self-contained and self-sufficient activity, but a mere segment of that trajectory which is the spiritual life as a whole. The aesthetic spirit, which from its own point of view is the pure negation of self-transcendence, is seen from the reflective point of view to have its very being in its self-transcendence, its passage from the life of art to another and a fuller life, from the monadic world of imagination to the world of reality whose essence is its transcendence of all monadism. This has always been seen by those who have regarded art as a means of education, an activity especially proper to children because a natural propaedentic to the intellectual life of maturity ; and some such view of art has been universally held by the greatest philosophers, both ancient and modern. But such a view would be misleading if it were taken to mean that art is nothing but a toy to be left behind in the nursery. There are two ways in which the peculiar value of art and beauty may be vindicated, and their claim to an essential place among the possessions of the human spirit defended : first, by insisting upon the aesthetic activity as it is in itself, by pointing out that beauty merely as beauty is an irreplaceable and infinitely precious possession, insufficient perhaps to fill the whole of life but yet admitting of no substitute that can even begin to console us for its loss ; and secondly, by pointing out that in the aesthetic activity we achieve a symbolic or imaginative vision of the universe, the premonition of a truth to be reached in its explicitness by science and philosophy. We may value art for what it says, because what it says is beautiful ; or for what it means, because what it means, but does not say, is true.

Neither vindication of the worth of art is true to the exclusion of the other. Beauty in itself, as an immediate and self-contained value, is certainly a thing without which the world would be poorer, a thing which nothing else can replace ; but that does not prove that we ought, on this or that given occasion or indeed ever, to pursue it when there is truth to pursue. We are still exposed to Plato's reluctant conclusion that art is an eye which must be plucked out if we are to enter the kingdom of heaven. On the other hand, to regard beauty as nothing but a confused vision of truth is to take the heart out of it, to treat the aesthetic experience as a necessary evil, a stage in the road towards truth which is valueless in itself and desirable only for its ultimate consequences. One view makes beauty a form of vice, the other a form of physic.

But though no ' apology for poetry ' can be based on either point of view taken separately, the convergence of the two gives us a conception of art for which no apology is needed. Art is the immediacy of experience; and though there can be no immediacy without implicit mediation, neither can there be mediation except as resting on and penetrated by immediacy. Imagination is not thought, and unless thought is present there can be no imagination: yet imagination is the focus, the luminous centre, of all thought. The attempt at a self-contained life of art is therefore of necessity futile. An art which hugs itself in the conviction of its own self-sufficiency and pretends to exist for its own sake is an illusion, and can only end by becoming invertebrate and unproductive. But as art actually exists, it exists not in this isolation, but in the closest union with thought; what has by thought been grasped becomes expressive, because immediate, in the form of art, and thus every achievement of every other phase of the spiritual life passes into art, there to be focused into a luminous point from which it can reissue into the explicitness of thought.

Thus art in itself is a phase of consciousness which is always being transcended; its instability involves it in a death which takes place not at a certain moment of development in the individual or the race, but at every moment. But in its relation to the spiritual life as a whole, art is immortal, and at every moment it is created anew in the shape of the immediate consciousness which the spirit has of itself, the ever-springing fountain-head of the spiritual life.

§ 30. *Art and its History.*—The particular forms which art assumes at any given period of human history are necessarily mortal. None of them is or can be a joy for ever. Not only are the individual poems and paintings of individual artists doomed to a merely material corruption, but they must become objects first of hatred and then of indifference to the world that has accepted them; its very enthusiasm for their beauty generates a revolt against themselves and the ideal for which they stand.

It is no more possible for an individual work of art to be thought beautiful for ever, than for an individual man to live for ever. But they await a resurrection, and some do not await it in vain. A time may come when people shall rediscover the beauty of this work, done by artists long dead, and value it not merely archaeologically but aesthetically. This interest in the art of distant ages is such a familiar thing in the modern world that we are apt to regard it as normal, and to forget that it is a thing of comparatively recent origin and comparatively small extent. It did not exist at all in the greatest period of the ancient world. The Greeks cared nothing for the art of their Minoan predecessors, or for the beauties of Egyptian sculpture. The Romans admired Greek work, but they regarded the Greeks rather as contemporaries, carrying on the tradition of the old masters, than as representing an age wholly removed from their own. It was not till that reverence for antiquity, which so strongly marked the spiritual life of the Middle Ages, had culminated in the Renaissance, that the modern faculty of admiring ancient art established itself. And even now this faculty is the fruit of special education, and only exists in a very small minority of people. Contemporary art is the only art whose appeal is direct and spontaneous ; and that is because it embodies imaginatively the experience of the contemporary world. We are all, though many of us are snobbish enough to wish to deny it, in far closer sympathy with the art of the music-hall and the picture-palace than with Chaucer and Cimabue, or even Shakespeare and Titian. By an effort of historical sympathy we can cast our minds back into the art of a remote past or an alien present, and enjoy the carvings of cavemen and Japanese colour-prints ; but the possibility of this effort is bound up with that development of historical thought which is the greatest achievement of our civilization in the last two centuries, and it is utterly impossible to people in whom this development has not taken place. The natural and primary aesthetic attitude is to enjoy contemporary art, to despise and dislike the art of the recent past, and wholly to ignore everything else.

But this resurrection of ancient art, effected by the growth of our modern historical consciousness, is not a revival of the past. That is impossible. We may read Chaucer with enjoyment, but we cannot be Chaucer ; our experience is not his experience, and therefore our imaginative outlook is not his. We see in Chaucer's poems something that he did not see there, and do not see what he saw there. And in many cases it is perfectly certain that the qualities which we admire in ancient works of art are the opposite of the qualities which their contemporaries enjoyed. A work whose greatness in its own day consisted in its paradoxical audacity is enjoyed to-day for its innocent conventionality by people who detest audacity and paradox ; and it is a typical irony that we should admire Greek statues for their whiteness.

What is true of individual works is true of styles and forms. Painting nowadays means painting easel-pictures ; but this is a recent innovation in the history of art, and not one that is likely to endure. The ballad, the play, the symphony, and all such forms, depend upon historical circumstances which cannot be permanent. The work of art itself is on a different level. What new forms it may take in the future, no one can pretend to know ;· we can only be certain that they will not be those which it has assumed in the past.

But the transformations which art undergoes in the course of its history are the expression not of a self-contained life of art which initiates its own new forms by a dialectic of its own, but of the life of the spirit as a whole. Art, as art, has no history. Art means the aesthetic activity, imagination : and imagination is the act of presenting to oneself a complete, self-contained, monadic world which exists only in and for that act. Every such act ignores every other; from the aesthetic point of view for which alone art exists as art, nothing exists except one individual work of art at any individual moment. From the historical point of view the work of art does not as such exist; all that exists is the imaginative act, and this imaginative act is seen as a resultant or expression of activities which are not imaginative. Hence there is no history of art; there is only the history of humanity. The force which transforms art from one shape to another as this history proceeds is not art, it is that force which reveals itself in history as a whole, the force of the spirit. Hence no event in the so-called history of art can be explained by reference to the principles of art itself. To explain the history of architecture, we must study the technique of building construction and the social purposes which buildings are intended to serve; to explain the history of music, we must study those forms of social organization which give rise to choirs and orchestras; to explain the history of painting, we must begin by asking what people have painted with, and upon what they have painted, and why. And no history of literature can begin to be history in the true sense of the word unless it is a history of religion, of science, of philosophy, and of ethical and political ideals.

What is commonly known as the history of art, just because it neglects these principles, is not history at all. It is a mere chronicle of facts whose connexion with each other is merely temporal and spatial. The task of history is to show why things happened, to show how one thing led to another. But one work of art does not lead to another; each is a closed monad, and from one monad to another there is no historical transition. Our ordinary histories of art are magic-lantern shows in which we are invited to contemplate first one work of art, and then another, and then another; as if an historian should think that he had discharged his whole duty when he had told us that this year there was an earthquake, next year a battle, and the year after that a famine.

The same is true of criticism. What is usually called criticism is the mere expression of opinion upon the aesthetic qualities of works of art ; it is in fact what in § 25 has been called appreciation. The true function of the art-critic is not simply to say that he likes this and dislikes that, but to explain works of art ; that is to say, to put people, including himself, in possession of information which will enable them to appreciate intelligently. Now a work of art as such cannot be explained ; it is self-explanatory or nothing. What can be explained is the process by which the artist reached this particular point of view. As has already been pointed out (§ 21) the title given to a work of art is an indication of this process, and is intended to enable others to repeat the process and so reach the point of view at which the work of art explains itself ; and the function of the critic is to do this on an extended scale. Hence the history and criticism of art are the same thing : namely the history of the human spirit in general, regarded as an activity of thought which, transcending the monadism of art, makes the advance of the aesthetic consciousness at once possible and intelligible.

SUGGESTIONS FOR FURTHER STUDY

It is impossible to become even tolerably competent in the philosophy of art without two qualifications : a training in art and a training in philosophy. (*a*) Every one enjoys to some extent the beauty of natural objects and works of art, and expresses his enjoyment in acts which are themselves works of art : but this does not entitle him to lay down the law about art. He must first develop and discipline his aesthetic powers by working long and seriously at the technical problems of some medium which should be that of music, painting, or the like, rather than the too familiar and therefore less instructive medium of words. Looking at pictures and listening to music are inadequate for this purpose : the student must learn to draw and compose. Without this artistic training, the philosophy of art must perish for lack of matter ; the philosopher is trying to reflect without having anything to reflect upon. This is an extremely common fault in the books written about art by philosophers and psychologists. The notion that it can be mended by psychological observation of other people's experiences is a childish blunder. (*b*) On the other hand, books written by people whose artistic experience is profound often fail through lack of training in philosophical thought. This training can only be acquired by general philosophical study, not by study of the philosophy of art taken by itself : a philosopher of art who is not competent in all branches of philosophy is necessarily incompetent in the philosophy of art. Our educational system makes it difficult for the same person to receive both these trainings : but not impossible.

Subject to these warnings, the following books may be mentioned as especially deserving the student's attention. The first group consists of introductory works, critical and historical.

1. CARRITT, *The Theory of Beauty* (Methuen, 5s., second edition). This is the best general introduction to the subject in English, and consists chiefly of critical discussions of the most important theories.

2. BOSANQUET, *History of Aesthetic* : or,

3. CROCE, *History of Aesthetic*, being Part II of his *Aesthetic* (English translation, second edition, Macmillan, 1922. The second edition alone is complete and trustworthy).

The second group comprises the chief landmarks in the history of thought on the subject.

4. PLATO, *Republic*, especially books II, III, X (translation Jowett).

5. ARISTOTLE, *Poetics* : see S. H. BUTCHER, *Aristotle's Theory of Poetry and Fine Art.*

6. VICO : see CROCE, *Giambattista Vico* (English translation).

7. KANT, *Critique of the Judgment* (English translation).

8. HEGEL, *Aesthetic* : the whole work translated by F. B. P. Osmaston (four volumes), the *Introduction* alone, with an introductory essay by the translator, by B. Bosanquet. A highly-compressed statement of Hegel's view as to the place of art in life is in his *Encyclopaedia*, §§ 556–563 (= WALLACE, *Hegel's Philosophy of Mind*, pp. 169–74).

9. CROCE, *Aesthetic* (see above). A more compact and mature statement of the view is in his *Breviario di Estetica*, translated under the title *The Essence of Aesthetics* in the volume *New Essays on Aesthetics*.

It is impossible here to say anything of the vast mass of books on art written by artists ; but such books are nearly always worth reading, though the views which they express are, as a rule, one-sided and exaggerated.

INDEX

Printed in England at the Oxford University Press